A meeting with sharks and cancer

Kim Ronaldson
© 2015

A Meeting with sharks and cancer.
Copyright © by Kim Ronaldson 2015

Published by Kim Ronaldson

ISBN   978-0-9935283-0-9

Author: Kim Ronaldson
Editor: Fiona Cowan
Cover design: Kim Ronaldson.

Where quotes are stated in the body of this book these are with the express permission of the person making that statement, their professional body and/or their employer.

This book has been compiled by the author by way of general information and guidance in relation to the subjects it addresses. It is not an alternative and is not to be relied upon as professional medical or pharmaceutical advice on any specific aspects of what this book covers.

You are strongly advised to consult your own medical practitioner.

To the best of the knowledge and belief of the author, all material and content is up to date as at 15th December 2015

The author and his publisher exclude (so far as the law allows) all and any liability arising directly or indirectly from the use or misuse of any of the information contained in this book.

About Kim Ronaldson

I was born in Lambeth, London on 18th July 1959, the first child of Terry and Frances Ronaldson. A couple of years later, we were joined by my sister Karen.

We lived in south London until I was thirteen years old, when we moved to Guildford in Surrey. I've lived there on and off ever since, in between living abroad for eleven and a half years.

I'm now married to the best person in the world, Hazel, and have two stepsons that live with us: Jack and Nathan.

My hobbies are scuba diving, skiing, motorcycles — both riding and watching. I also love sailing, and one of the greatest adrenaline rushes ever was flying helicopters. I read a lot and I have a passion for all sorts of music, especially classical music.

I kept a daily diary from the time I got home from hospital; for the first year I recorded blood pressure, heart rate, temperature and oxygen saturation. I also made notes about the day, be it good or bad. I will quote verbatim from the diary from time to time.

Foreword

Kim, Hazel,

Thank you for the privilege of reading this, a wonderfully moving but calm and thoughtful book. It's clear you have managed the kidney cancer in the same organised, logical and considerate way you have managed your personal and work life previously.

There are some really nice observations around the bewildering news around the diagnosis and how after the surgery you felt uneasy because you assumed you would almost be "obliged" to feel ill.

I think your motivation and thirst for insights into the disease have definitely helped you manage the burden of the medication and the "shadow" of frequent scans.

It's a great tribute to you and Hazel that you have had the strength to truly move forward after your diagnosis, with a thriving business, new skills and directions.

Your experiences will be highly appreciated by very many patients and their families I have no doubt.

All the best, H.

Professor Hardev Pandha MB ChB (Birm), FRACP, FRCP, PhD, CSST (Medical Oncology)

Dedication

This book is dedicated to the most special person on the planet, my beautiful wife Hazel.

Acknowledgements

Obviously Hazel, my Mum, my sister Karen, niece Ciara, my stepsons Jack and Nathan and a myriad of other family members and friends. It's very special when people come and see you from lands near and far to see how you are.

To my 'teams', Mr Neil Barber from Urology Partners and his team, Professor Hardev Pandha and his team. To the Spire Clare Park Hospital for allowing me to use the scans in this book. To the doctors and staff at Frimley Park Hospital. The staff at Nuffield Health Care and St Luke's Cancer centre both in Guildford.

To the management and staff at Tullett Prebon plc and to Nigel Lewis-Baker MBE, the trustees, patrons and supporters of Topic of Cancer.

Finally, a thank you to everybody who's cared for me and my condition. Your support and interest have been, and continue to be, motivation beyond belief.

Introduction

This was never the book I was planning to write. But life has some funny twists, so this is the book I'm now writing.

I hope it helps you if you have just been diagnosed with cancer, are living with cancer or know somebody with cancer. You feel like you have fallen into a dark abyss when you're told, but there is a light at the end of the tunnel, a very bright light. All you have to do is open your eyes and work, walk and plan towards it.

In many ways, sharks and cancer are two things we really *don't* want to encounter in life time. But read on and you will see why both can be encountered and survived.

Among these pages you will read a story — my story — and how I've ended up writing this book. It contains the good, the bad and the ugly. It is honest and it hurt to write, often taking me days to get over what I wanted to tell you.

Cancer is a big word with very big implications.
Hope is a bigger, better word... and I like hope!

Kim Ronaldson
www.first-aid-development.co.uk
www.kimnosis.com
www.topicofcancer.org.uk

December 2015

Chapters.

and cancer

Prologue.

Sitting in a surgeon's office accompanied by my wife Hazel, the computer screen in front of us, was not my ideal day out. It was obvious that the scan staring out at us had a problem — a large problem, and it was mine. It showed the chest area and abdomen and on the right hand side of me there was a mass. Even to my untrained eye it looked wrong.

The surgeon started to speak which broke my gaze; Hazel's eyes remained locked to that image.

Did I know before he spoke that I had cancer? Maybe, because I'd asked my own GP and she wouldn't rule it out. Did I think I had cancer when I looked at that screen? Yes, I was convinced before I was told.

I had already played this event out in my mind before the appointment with the surgeon and now I could see the 'alien' in front of me, there was only one more Get Out Of Jail Free card; it *might* be benign.

Could it possibly be benign? It looked massive, and the chance of that was very quickly dispelled. The surgeon, with all his experience, was 100 per cent convinced it was cancerous. I thought that diagnosis was it. It wasn't. There was more.

You feel like you are staring into a big black hole when the words come out — *you have kidney cancer*. Our world darkened further when we were also told there were a further eight tumours and that we had a big fight on our hands.

I gathered my thoughts quickly and started asking questions. I wanted and needed to know everything, and I still do.

Do I have answers? Some; but more than that, I have a story I want to tell you. I hope you find strength in it, if you need strength. I hope you find amusement in it, because there have been some very amusing moments and mostly, I hope you enjoy reading it.

Chapter One

How it started

In September 2012 Hazel and I were invited to a wedding in Sri Lanka. It was a customer's wedding and we were both very excited for a number of reasons. Firstly, we had never been to Sri Lanka or anywhere in that area, we had never attended a Muslim wedding before, we were going to spend a couple of weeks after the wedding touring Sri Lanka, and finally, we were going to scuba dive in the clear warm waters of the Indian Ocean.

Looking back, it was probably the first time I noticed a swelling under my ribs. When we landed in Colombo my ribs were very sore and I was convinced I'd slept awkwardly on the plane. I didn't really check or notice anything untoward. When you've been on a plane for ten hours and slept for plenty of them, you can get a bit cramped and sore. I didn't pay it much attention. Why would I? I felt fit and we were in a new country having an adventure.

We had a heap of luggage with us as it was a multi-leg trip: formal attire for the wedding, all the scuba gear; and comfortable clothes for a tour of Sri Lanka. We spent a total of twenty hours in various taxis on some of the most outrageously dangerous roads in the world.

The wedding was great, the holiday was great and really interesting, and the diving was spectacular. We were in high spirits and I was feeling good emotionally and physically.

We returned to the UK and life continued.

I was working as a money broker in the City of London for a company called Tullett Prebon. I'd been in the money market as a broker for thirty-one years by then. I'd lived in London, New York, Sydney and Singapore and was back in London again after eleven and a half years in those countries, the longest stint being in Australia. During my time there I proudly became an Australian citizen, and I'm now a dual citizen of the planet.

My work day started at 4.30am when the alarm went off. I've always got up easily so I was straight into the shower and shave, and out of the door by 5.00am. I was at my desk in the city by 6.00am and immediately started trading. In later years I'd been trading Australian and New Zealand dollars, hence the early starts. For the most part, my day finished at 5.00pm when I would make my way home. As a money broker I entertained customers from time to time, mostly in the evenings, as lunch time 'entertainment' had become a thing of the past.

I rode a motorcycle to work every day as it afforded me flexibility. Summers were fun, winters were cold, but I enjoyed the ride — especially home in the evenings, which was a chance to reflect on the day's events.

It wasn't until early 2013 that the ache under my ribs troubled me again. I'd previously fractured a couple of ribs in the same place where I was now feeling sore: once while boxing, and once after crashing on my motorcycle while taking part in a track day at Brands Hatch. Was the ache just an ache, or an indication of something more than merely sore ribs?

My general health at the time was very good indeed. We'd been skiing with no problems. At the time I was an active scuba diver and dive instructor, and a first aid instructor. I was perhaps a little overweight, but no obvious health problems.

Looking back, and there's been a bit of that happening recently, I did have an annoying stubborn cough that wouldn't go away. A couple of people had mentioned the cough. My mother thought it was a nervous cough and my brother-in-law nicknamed me 'Bob Fleming' as I never seemed to be able to clear my throat properly.

By April 2013, I could now feel and became aware of an obvious swelling on my right side, just below my ribs. I thought it might be my liver as I had an active social life and entertained customers a lot; most of the time, if I overdid anything it would be alcohol.

I stopped drinking any alcohol for a couple of weeks, which didn't bother me at all. I was expecting the swelling to recede but it didn't. If anything, it seemed to be getting bigger. In real terms it probably wasn't but I was becoming very conscious that maybe there was a problem.

In early May 2013 I went to see my local doctor and told her about the swelling under my ribs. She examined me and, without a second thought, she ordered an ultrasound scan and a blood test.

The gravity of the situation was not uppermost in my mind — although, deep down, I knew a large swelling under my ribs could be either a tumour or a buggered liver. It was in the area of my liver and a tumour could be cancerous.

I told Hazel, but played it down to everybody else. I wasn't going to say anything until I knew something more specific about the ultrasound and blood tests.

Temple in Colombo

The stunning view of the Candy hill side.

Chapter Two

The tests

My local GP, ordered the required tests: the blood tests were done at the Royal Surrey County Hospital (RSCH) on 26th April 2013, as was the ultrasound, later that day at the Jarvis Centre in Guildford.

I've always had a great interest in medicine and human biology and I tried to make out the ultrasound image, but I couldn't. The nurse who did it and wrote the report didn't give anything away, either visually or verbally. I would have to wait until my local doctor received the results and we could discuss them.

After a week I returned to see my local doctor and she was very concerned. The ultrasound had found an inflamed kidney and a couple of other minor problems. At this point there was no mention of a tumour. The greater concern were the blood test results. There's a test called an ESR test (Erythrocyte Sedimentation Rate) which is a non-specific indication of inflammation in the body. A normal range for a man of my age was less than twenty; mine was ninety-four!

The Doctor explained very calmly that when she had studied medicine, the ESR was used as a diagnosis for kidney cancers although, subsequently, newer tests have proved more reliable as have CT scans.

I asked the question which was dominating my thoughts now: *Do I have cancer*? She didn't commit herself, and instead explained that it really needed to be investigated further. But she did concede that cancer couldn't be ruled out.

She ordered an interview at the RSCH for 13th May 2013, and a talk with a specialist urology nurse.

At this point, I was becoming ever more aware that the tumour, or swelling, or whatever you want to call it, was not just going to go away. Best case, it was a benign tumour. Worst case, it could be cancer, as the doctor had suggested.

The specialist urology nurse said I would have to have a CT scan so I changed tack a bit at this point, to speed things up, and made the most of the fact that I had private medical cover through my employer. I was referred to Mr. Neil Barber, an urologist, at the Spire Clare Park Hospital in Farnham.

My work colleagues for the most part were unaware that I was having all these tests. I fudged over it with afternoons off or a sick day here or there. Not even my family were totally aware of the situation. They knew I'd been for tests but I really had played the whole situation down. I didn't want to worry everybody if it was going to turn out as something lesser, rather than major.

Hazel and I met up with the consultant, Mr. Neil Barber, on 16th May 2013 in his rooms at Clare Park.

As we walked in he already had my scan on the computer screen and even my untrained eye I could see there was a lump that didn't belong.

As you can see below (circled) on the left lower side of this X-ray, there's a large tumour pushing on other organs — that was our first view of the alien.

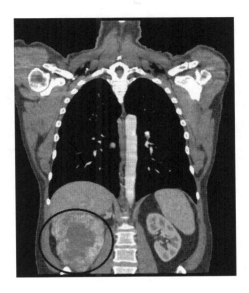

Reproduced with the kind permission of Spire Clare Park hospital

We looked at the scan and several different shots from the CT scans, and in that instant our world changed. Life would never be the same again. *What will happen? What's the prognosis? Am I going to die and, if so, when? What's to be done, when and how?* A million questions blasted through my head all at the same time. It was like staring into a big black hole... and this was the view of my world at that moment:

Neil Barber is an expert in kidney cancer; he's straight talking, but with a manner which allowed us to ask the most simple or complicated questions. His answers were compassionate but to the point.

He was very open and obviously had plenty of experience in dealing with the Mr. and Mrs. Ronaldson's of this world. The good news was that we liked him from the outset and felt comfortable with his explanations, which was comforting.

We sat quietly while he pointed at the screen with medical explanations of the results from the CT scan. Early in the conversation he confirmed what I had most feared: it *was* cancer. But I felt better for knowing. That may seem odd — but after weeks of thinking it could be or it couldn't be, what if, what if not... in a bizarre way I was relieved to know. Most importantly, I now wanted to learn what was to be done; how and when?

Hazel was very upset and shocked. Both Neil and I comforted her, tissues at the ready. We were both completely stunned.

Even though I was upset, I wanted to know absolutely everything. What I was up against, the odds, the operation, the recovery and ongoing treatment. Most of all, I needed to know who the enemy was, what was the 'alien' growing inside me that was trying to kill me.

Neil said that through his experience it looked to be about one kilogramme in weight, fifteen centimetres mass. That's slightly larger than a tennis ball. He looked through the various images of the CT scan and formed the initial impression that the tumour was a primary kidney tumour and had not metastasized (advanced to other parts of the body), which is also known as secondary cancer.

While he spoke to us the report from the radiologist arrived and the bad news got dramatically worse.

He had just explained that the tumour would most probably come away cleanly and there would be no need for any further treatment. His face darkened considerably when he read to us that I had a further six kidney cancers in my lungs and two kidney cancers in lymph nodes just beside the split in the bronchi and my liver. Our entire being sank. I've never known an intensity of emotion like I felt on that day. It felt like I was looking into an emotional abyss. For poor Hazel, if you can imagine, it must have been even worse.

Now is a good time to clarify something in case, like me, you're not an oncologist, doctor or medically trained. I had/have cancer in my lungs and lymph nodes. They are not lung cancers or lymph cancers. They are called secondary, metastases or advanced cancers, but they are all *kidney cancers*.

I asked how or why I had cancer. Was it from my father who'd died of cancer or was it due to alcohol consumption? No to both, inasmuch as there was no apparent link to either. He did ask if I smoked, which I never have. You start to think of all the things that you've done in the past that might have caused it. That is a waste of time and energy of course, as the tumour is there now and whatever has happed in the past makes no difference — you can't go back in time and change it.

Here's an extract from Mr. Barber's report back to the urology nurse specialist at the Royal Surrey County Hospital and to my local GP:

"As you know, he was known for some time to have a raised ESR, but more recently thought he could feel a lump in the right side of his tummy. An ultrasound scan confirmed a likely lesion and he went on to have a CT scan of the chest and abdomen here at Clare Park Hospital yesterday, which has unfortunately confirmed a 15cm mass arising from the right kidney. Furthermore, our radiologist informed them that the scan demonstrated enhanced necrotic right hilar and sub carinal nodes, the largest one measuring 2.4cm in short axis, with a number of smaller nodules in both lungs, the largest in the right upper lobe measuring 8mm. There is extensive filling of a large number of tumour vessels, both from the hilar route and the gondal."

For those who want to understand more about cancers that move from the original site, the best and most valuable analogy I've heard in explanation of secondary, advanced or metastatic cancer is as follows:

If you had a mighty oak tree and you took some clippings, you could plant the saplings on the other side of the planet. As long as the growing conditions were right, they would grow and flourish.
If you then destroyed the mighty oak, the oak saplings elsewhere would still continue to grow into other mighty oak trees. The same can be applied to cancer. The primary cancer may go, but the secondary cancers thrive in the right conditions by

themselves. Secondary cancers and the reasons they move from the primary site are complicated.

Neil explained the options, which were pre-operative chemo followed by a nephrectomy (kidney removal) or, in my case, a nephrectomy followed by chemo. He explained what needed to be done and how things would proceed. I listened attentively while Hazel just stared at the screen trying to take in all that had been said in the last few minutes.

It is really difficult to describe my emotions at that point. It is strange enough seeing the inside of a human body — but seeing your own, and with such an obvious tumour that if left to its own devices, would kill me sooner than later is, to say the least, a game changer. Hazel has said it, and I agree: that image will never leave us.

The conversation was among us all, but we were totally led by Mr. Barber. It seemed to me then, and it's more than confirmed now, that there was only one way to deal with this 'alien', and that was to get rid of it ASAP and deal with the mini 'aliens' afterwards.

So, the plan was set. Neil was to organise a radical nephrectomy. 'Radical' meaning to open me up, not keyhole surgery; and 'nephrectomy'; as mentioned, meaning kidney removal.
Neil wanted to complete this over two days, which was a new way of dealing with this sort of operation. Day one is to embolise the tumour (stop blood flow to the tumour) and day two, the removal of the 'alien'.

The reason for the removal to be done over two days was that the embolisation on day one should radically reduce blood loss on the day of the removal, and make the operation easier and safer. That works for me!

It was left to Neil to organise dates and we asked what *we* should do. What do you do to help the situation? It was all so much to take in and we really didn't know what was going to happen. After all, what do you do when you've just been told you have multiple cancers?

He said we should carry on as we were, and just to keep as healthy as I could. I needed to be in the best possible health for the surgery. We told him were we were meant to be leaving on a ferry that day to go to France on the motorcycle. We were planning to ride to Le Mans, catch up with friends there and watch a weekend of motorcycle racing. Without a blink, he told us to *still* get on a ferry, go to France, enjoy the MotoGP and leave everything up to him.

There is a very amusing aside to the conversation with Neil Barber in his officer that day and I hope he's laughed at it as much as we have.
The explanation for the title of the book you are reading right now, and why we actually laughed at this most trying of times, is at the end of this book...
After a long, in depth, interesting and distressing conversation, we left his office and drove home. We cried in the car park, on the drive home, and a lot

ever since. And now came the even more difficult part — telling people.

Chapter Three

The (very) difficult part

I have a large and close family, where aunts, uncles and cousins feel just like additional mums, dads, brothers and sisters. I've also married into a large family — there are seventeen family members closely related to Hazel. We are both very close to our families and we have a wide group of brilliant friends.

In addition I have two stepsons Jack and Nathan; how were they going to take this news? After all, they were going to be the people closest to me and their mother, regardless of the outcome.

How do you break it to people you love that you have advanced cancer? On the drive around to my mum's after the diagnosis, I rehearsed and rehearsed what I was going to say. I'd do the same thing again many times before telling other family and friends. Did all the rehearsals work? Of course not; my emotions always got the better of me.

I did try and keep a clear and logical head and repeated the diagnosis verbatim every time as best I could. Most times my explanation would be interrupted by either me or the person I was talking to breaking down.

It was a difficult thing to explain, because I was still trying to get my own head around it.

Cancer is a shocker of a word. For far too long now, people have equated Cancer with Death — and it's *not* always like that. As you will see.

From the moment you are born, you're starting to die. When and how is what we are most concerned about I guess. As soon as you add *cancer* to a sentence, people think the worst.

My father died of multiple cancers. I have friends and family with cancer. I've lost friends to cancer and, as they say, cancer touches us all. It touched me a little bit too much. But, when you widen your thoughts, you realise that you lose people all through your life to many different things. However, cancer is still the bad guy.

I went around to my mum's — my sister and niece were there too — and as I pulled up in front of her house I knew that I had to go in and tell them. But I didn't even want to get out of the car. I did the best I could. It was a struggle to get it across that I had secondary kidney cancer, but that it wasn't the end of the world. I tried my best to explain that there was a plan and, even though it wasn't good situation, there was hope and the urologist was positive.

It is very difficult to purvey a positive sentiment to people when you've just dropped such a bombshell. I'm sure most of what I was saying didn't sink in. The fact I had just told them I had cancer was all they were focused on at this point.

How did I feel inside? Torn apart. I didn't want to put all of these people through such an emotional ride. We all have our aches and pains, problems and hurdles, to get over. I wanted to run away, not from the cancer or the looming operations, but from *people*. I didn't want people to be upset, scared or worried about me. I wasn't scared, I didn't even feel ill, but I certainly didn't want to put this on other people.

The truth is that love is a two-way thing and, if somebody loves you, they want to be there to support you and help in any way they can. The problem for the most part is *how*? What can people do for you? Nothing, in many ways, just be there for you. And they have been, in bucket loads! Every inch of the bastard way.

Mum and I cried together for a long time. I'd not seen her so upset for many years. I felt hopeless and empty. I now realise that the emotion of cancer is much, much worse than the physical problems of cancer. I can only speak about my own experience: one thing I've learned is that every person who has cancer has 'their' cancer. It's very personal.

The other thing you realise is that your relationships with people can change. You are not treated the same any more. I feel sometimes that I'm being handled with kid gloves — but I've also come to understand that people can only look at you from their world as they understand it. They worry and get as upset as I do, but with the added frustration that they want to be able to *do* something, anything to make you better. And of course they can't.

Chapter Four

The long wait

The Long Wait is what I call the bit between the diagnosis and the operations to start dealing with it. That seemed so *long*.

In the interim, I spent hours researching anything and everything to do with kidney cancers — the good, the bad and the spectacularly ugly. There's certainly a lot of information on the internet. Some of it is helpful and some of it is not to be trusted at all.

I just needed to know. Instinctively I felt that I would gain strength physically by being mentally prepared from the knowledge. It's not the same for everybody, as I've discovered. Some people want to totally ignore what's behind the problem and just get on with their treatment. Some go into complete denial and pretend it's not there at all. For me though, it was all about getting to know everything that I possibly could. I had to know the enemy and everything and anything I could use to fight it.

The day I was diagnosed was when I started breaking the news to my family and friends. It really upsets me, recalling the conversations and phone calls I made. I had to space them out, to give me a chance to recover my composure between each call.

The reactions to my bombshell were surprisingly varied — but they were all concerned, worried, frightened and feeling totally and utterly useless. Much the same as we felt ourselves, in fact.

Cancer: a big word with massive implications, it's true. But it amazed me then, as it does today, that people are so scared of that *word*. People sometimes still whisper the word cancer to me or just ask vaguely about my 'health'. Some people try to just say 'C', perhaps hoping that if they don't mention cancer in full it will make it better or it will go away. It's cancer, a disease like of other diseases — and they too can kill you.

You wouldn't hear a newsreader say: "Here's the news. Today a man died of Ebola [whispered] and a women was knocked off her bike by a bus [whispered] and died at the scene".

It is what it is, there's no magical answer, and not talking about it makes it worse. Talk about it, get it out there, go and get checked.

As you've already read, we were due to go to Le Mans on the motorcycle to watch the French round of MotoGP. After Neil telling us to go, we bit the bullet, sorted out another train to Calais and left early the next day.

Hazel's brother Bryan and his wife Lorraine had delayed their departure to travel with us if we were still going, hoping for good news. Sadly, the good news didn't happen.

We were all packed, met up with Bryan and Lorraine and rode to Folkstone to get the train to Calais. On a motorcycle you really need to concentrate. My world and the best person in the world, Hazel, sit on that bike. The bike is in my hands along with our lives and our future. I had no interest in putting any of that in danger.

On the way to France

We left early the next day, the four of us on two motorcycles making our way to France. It was surreal to say the least. Less than twenty-four hours before, I had been diagnosed with nine cancer tumours and was awaiting news about the operation. Now here we were on a train under the English Channel going on holiday.

I concentrated hard on the road while Hazel and I spoke together through the helmet intercom system. It was good in a way, as I could take a break from the cancer thoughts, but it also gave me time to reflect and prepare for... what, exactly? That's the point: I didn't know. It's difficult to express or convey the emotions. Bryan and Lorraine were brilliant as riding companions; very open, concerned and honest about the cancer.

We rode all day without too much adventure and arrived late afternoon at the hotel where we were staying. The hotel was about ten miles from the track. Actually, there was one little mishap. At one point Bryan and Lorraine were leading and we lost them, the bikes separated on the road. I stopped to turn around and retrace my route back to a common point where we'd last seen them. I went up a hill, pulled the bike to the right and then tried to turn it around on the cambered road. Hazel asked if she should get off, I said no and made the turn. Well, made half a turn — lost my balance on the camber of the road and the hill and had to lay the bike down.

I managed to hold the weight for a while on one leg, but the three hundred-plus kilograms of the fully laden bike, plus the combined weight of Hazel and myself, was too much. Down we all went. It happened in slow motion and was quite comedic. I hit the ground and Hazel followed, landing squarely... on the alien.

We were both fine, just felt a little stupid as we picked ourselves up off the road. The alien didn't seem to be in any way changed. The bike was hardly marked.

I would like to thank all the local French people who stopped to help us. The French are far more motorbike friendly than the English generally are. There must have been quite a burst of adrenaline because I managed to pick up the bike and its load in one go.

A couple of minutes later we did indeed catch up with our riding companions. They were as amused about our crash as we were.

We met up later on the Friday afternoon at the hotel with friends — Nick, his wife Carolyn, Stephen and his wife Tanya, and another mate, Barry, who had all ridden down on their bikes the day before.

It was an emotional get-together but they treated us as they'd always treated us and, apart from the fact that I'd stopped drinking, the trip was pretty normal. However, whatever happened, wherever we were, the 'alien' and his chums were always hovering in the background. Thinking back, it reminds me of when my father passed. Even though I was back to work after a week, he was perpetually in my waking and sleeping thoughts (and still is). Likewise, there was no escape from the cancer.

In all, we had a good safe trip and everybody was great. I was open with them, as I have been with everybody all the way through this.

Neil Barber said something to me which I carry as a mantra: "A positive mental attitude will get you through." How very true that is, and I can't count how many times I have said the same to others.

When we returned from France I had to tell the rest of my friends, customers (many of whom had become friends) and colleagues, and then start to make arrangements for some time off. I had a lot of people to tell and I was determined to tell them all personally. I worked in the financial markets and, as in all markets, rumours are rife. I wanted people to hear from the horse's mouth what was going on.

It was no easier telling non-family members than it had been with the family. I really struggled with it and one day I had to give up on the calls, emotionally exhausted. I started again the next day.

Finally, everybody knew as much as we did. It was then a case of waiting for my operation dates to come around. I spent the time reading up on foods that are good for your kidneys. You have to love the internet!

My return to work helped to an extent to take my mind off the cancer, but only for a short time.

Chapter Five

Cancer is —?

In this chapter I want to explain to you in simple terms about cancer. There's a lot of rubbish published about cancer and plenty of people will tell you how to 'cure' it.

As you already know, I'm not a doctor or a medic. At the time of my diagnosis I was a money broker, a qualified scuba instructor and first aid instructor. Although I have always been interested in medicine, I am not medically trained.

What *is* cancer then? What are these tumours we read so much about, that kill our friends and loved ones? Where do you go for information? Here's what I found, in plain language:

Your body replenishes its cells constantly. By the time you finish reading this sentence, fifty million of your cells will have died and been replaced by new ones. Regeneration is happening all the time. When one of the trillions of cells in your body is replaced, but there is a mutation in that cell, that cell will replicate and quickly multiply — this is what we call cancer. As the cells increase in number, we call that a tumour.

So, cancer is *part of you*. You can't catch it and it's not passed on to you. Therein lies the problem.

Your defence system is amazing. It fights off disease and it repairs breaks, cuts and bruises. But it doesn't recognise cancer as a problem because cancer is part of you; albeit a mutated cell, it's still one of your own cells. And cancer is clever.

The cancer cells have a 'stop' signal, as do your normal cells. This is to stop the white blood cells killing them. If your normal cells didn't have these 'stop' signs, then more tissue would be killed. This is what happens with the autoimmune diseases like diabetes, thyroid and Multiple Sclerosis.

The army of white blood cells that defend you constantly pass by the cancer, as it divides and multiplies, because it doesn't recognise it as being alien. The problem with cancer, and this is where it is clever, is that it multiplies quickly and sets up its own blood supply and can start taking nutrients and oxygen to aid its growth.

Some cancers are slow growing and others are very fast. I asked Neil Barber how long I'd had cancer. "A while," he said. I questioned him further and he said a long time, maybe years, many years. I was dumbfounded. After further enquiries with him and my oncologist, Professor Pandha, they suggested that the cancer could have started to form more than five years before I knew anything about it.

You will read that more and more people are being diagnosed with cancer; the 'cancer epidemic', as some headlines like to report it. That's true to some extent, but let's just break that headline down.

Firstly, cancer has been around forever. As soon as a cell divides it can mutate into a cancer cell. They have now found evidence of cancer in some very old bones, thousands of years old.

We are not the only animals that get cancer. Far from it. A lot of animals get cancer too, not just the animals we've domesticated. The thing is, humans have a longer life expectancy these days and as such, cancer has longer to develop. Logically, there is more time for cells to mutate and become a cancerous tumour, the older we get.

Some of us also have very bad lifestyles which could possibly contribute to getting cancer. Wild animals don't eat processed foods, don't drink alcohol and don't smoke, yet some of them still get cancer. Some animals do pass cancer on to others of their breed. Luckily, this isn't the case for humans.

Over the years, and with the advent of better technology, we have discovered more and varied cancers — more than two hundred different types.

When you read the headlines about the plague of cancers, just keep this in mind: there are now over seven billion humans on the planet, and that alone means more people are being diagnosed. We also understand more about cancers now, and as such, we can identify cancers that we didn't know about even five years ago.

The best news is that more people live with cancer than die of it these days. In the UK alone there are two and a half million cancer survivors. All of this information can be found online.

The big question about cancer is *why*. Why do the cells mutate? What damage is there to the DNA? What's causing the change? Those questions are still to be answered and there are plenty of top minds working on it. Later in the book I will update you about the latest developments regarding cancer research and some publications that I've referred to.

One of the problems is that your mutated cells may re-mutate, making the 'cure' a constantly moving target. You develop a drug to fight a mutated cancer cell and it works well on the original mutated cell. But the cells may have mutated again and, in effect, you're not treating the original set of mutated cells, you now have another different mutation which may not be affected by the drugs you're using. Even the mutated cells can mutate. I cannot overstate: cancer cells are clever, very clever.

Chapter Six

Operations time

There were, you may recall, to be two of them over two days, on 14th and 15th June 2013. I'm not going to go into any gory details so don't be afraid to read on. I will share just an overview from my own perspective.

I was to be operated on by Neil Barber and his team at Frimley Park Hospital. He suggested that I went for a new procedure whereby on the first day, the major tumour was 'embolised' (the blood flow is stopped), and on the second day the tumour removed via a radical (rather than keyhole) operation.

The reasoning behind the two days was that, if the tumour with its rich supply of blood was embolised then the removal would be safer, quicker and there would be significantly less blood loss. I can't remember the exact figures, but without the embolisation there could have been six litres of blood loss; as it was, I lost only one litre.

Hazel and I went to Frimley Park Hospital to check into my room for the next ten days. They were very good at the hospital and I would like to thank all the staff there for their help and care.

It was time for the first operation to start.

The porters came to collect me and I had to say goodbye to the most special person in the world — Hazel. On this first goodbye I wasn't all that emotional, maybe because I was going to be awake. Or maybe the gravity of the situation had yet to sink in.

I was given an epidural injection in my back that numbed me pretty much everywhere below the ribcage, which felt strange to say the least. I didn't like the epidural being put in at all. I'd had one before for a back problem, which was no fun, but I have to admit they do the job they are meant to. In the big picture that discomfort was nothing really, since it meant that I would be awake throughout the first operation while they were basically killing a major organ inside me. On *that* basis, I was very pleased to have it.

Totally numb, I was taken into the operating theatre and met by a team of surgeons and assistants, who were to perform the first operation, along with the anaesthetist and nurses. They set up the live X-ray machines and began embolising the tumour.

Since I was awake and conscious, and could see what they were doing on a screen, I was talking and asking plenty of questions. There was a problem though. I needed to keep very still throughout and I still had that pesky long term cough. The doctor asked me several times to stop coughing. I tried but I couldn't, which was problematic for him. The anaesthetist stepped in and injected me with something which quelled the cough for the moment. Where had he been for the past months and months when I couldn't get rid of that damn cough?

It was surreal as I was being operated on via the femoral artery on my right leg, and I was watching it and felt excited. I say *excited* for two reasons: this was the beginning of my treatment and getting better, plus I was able to watch it all. I am fascinated by the whole medical world, so watching any kind of operation up close and personal was a remarkable opportunity.

Job done and an excellent one, inasmuch as it achieved what was expected in just three hours or so. The doctors were pleased. They stopped the bleeding from the artery and glued it; very neat and tidy, I must say.

The excellent staff put up with a lot of questions from me. I deeply appreciated their input and professionalism at all times. Once the first operation was over they took me to the intensive care unit (ICU) as I had to be monitored. After all, they had stopped the blood supply to a major organ/tumour and, as such, parts of my insides were starting to die.

I was very comfortable in the ICU and was constantly attended to and checked over. There were some very sick people in there. I felt sorry for some of them as they were obviously in a very bad way. At least *I'd* started on the road to recovery.

I slept well. Hazel left late and returned early the next morning. Neil Barber came in and made sure we were both OK and ready for the next phase. I was and I wanted it to be over and done with. The big alien was soon going to be gone and we could then set about the other aliens.

For the second time I had to say goodbye to Hazel and this time I really struggled. It was bad enough that the day before she'd spent almost three and a half hours in my hospital room alone, not knowing what was going on. Today was the big one though, and again I was leaving her alone. I said an emotional goodbye to Hazel, feeling upset. I felt sorry for her and everybody I loved. I felt desperately useless. For me it was easy in a way: I was to be knocked out and I would awake some hours later when it was over. Everybody else just had to wait and wait.

Later in the book Hazel has added *her* story and what all of this was like from her perspective. During the first operation I was awake and totally engrossed in what was going on; for the second operation I was out cold. For Hazel though, during both operations she had to just sit and wait, I can't imagine what that must have been like.

Having a general anaesthetic is inherently dangerous. It is something that should always be avoided if at all possible. I really don't understand people who choose to have plastic surgery and procedures that are cosmetic, especially when it involves having general anaesthetic.

I was wheeled from the ICU into the area where they gave me the pre-med; needles in and a couple of breaths of oxygen and I was gone. The sleep under these drugs is black for me. I was now in the hands of Neil and his team.

About four hours later I awoke in the ICU, looked at the clock and pinched myself (somewhere I could feel!). I was alive and in one piece, minus one alien, and plus one eleven-inch scar.

I asked to see Hazel and she came in. I've never been so happy to see anybody in my entire life. She gave me an incredible boost of strength then, and continues to do so now. You would have to ask her how I was because, apart from the obvious, I felt fine and was now looking forward to taming the rest of the alien nation that was trying to take over my body.

Neil came to see me and described the operation as 'unremarkable' (good news). However in his later report he would have to say that there was a complication, as I had left the operating table with a lung infection. I didn't think this was fair, as I'd had a lung infection *before* the operation. The six kidney cancers in my lungs were obviously not helping pre- or post-operatively. In real terms I was on oxygen all the time because the oxygen level in my blood dropped a little low without it. All other stats returned to normal-ish quite quickly.

Neil said he would come in from time to time and see how I was doing, and we could talk over the operation. As ever, I had plenty of questions.

So, two operations done and both very successful. It was time to tell everybody. I got permission to use a phone and called my mum and sister, inviting them up to see me. They would call the rest of the family, but they declined the invitation to visit and I don't blame them. I phoned my aunt on my father's side and my brother and sister in law. Hazel said I was like Tigger. I was very determined to let everybody know how well I was.

Bryan and Lorraine did come up to see me, bless them. I thought it was brave as an ICU isn't the nicest place and Bryan, especially, felt uncomfortable in there. The good news for me, and indeed Bryan, was that I was only kept in ICU for a couple of hours before they felt I was stable enough to return to my room. After a few hours Bryan and Lorraine left, followed by Hazel, when I needed to sleep. Now it was time for me to set about getting better.

Pain? There was some, but modern drugs are great at pain management and I still had the epidural in. It's very strange being wired up to bleeping machines, cannulas in your hands and a catheter in your winkle (that's a medical term, by the way). The team of nurses, both in ICU and on the ward where my room was, were all great.

They expected me to be in hospital for up to ten days, but I started to set myself goals early on: home in five days and back to work in three months. One thing that has really given me strength is setting goals and making plans. I wanted to be home in five days, I wanted to be well enough to return to work in three months and as for the other cancers? They were NOT going to kill me. I was going to kill them!

Chapter Seven

Recovery time in hospital

I was operated on in Frimley Park Hospital, which is an NHS Trust hospital, although I was in a private room because I had medical insurance at the time. I've always been a fan of our National Health Service, although I accept it's not always perfect. In my case, the support that I received both in the private sector and NHS from the doctors and ever-attentive nurses was as good as it could have been. I thank them — *really* thank them.

It was coming to the end of the operation day. Everybody left that evening and I had a sandwich, plenty of liquid, and set about the sleeping thing. For those who know me well, they know sleeping is sometimes a bit of a challenge for me. I'm not good at sleeping. I do sleep, I sleep very well, but only for short periods.

That said, the nurses woke me every hour to take readings, make sure the epidural was still working and that I was OK. I looked a sight: stockings (surgical ones!) and around them a set of inflatable leg wraps that kept the blood circulating in my lower limbs and a bed that pulsed.

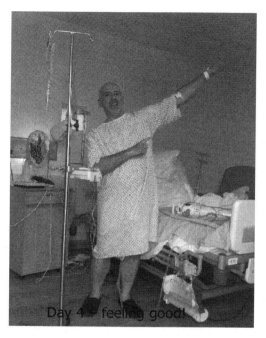
Day 4 - feeling good!

Morning two was the same as evening one. The usual round of tests and emptying of the Louis Vuitton bag (that's what we named the catheter bag used to test kidney output). I only had one kidney left and it was working overtime. I had to have the bag connected because the epidural was still in — and without the catheter, it would have all been very messy.

It seems as though only one kidney had been working for a while, because the cancerous tumour had probably hampered or destroyed the right kidney's function. There was very little of it showing when the tumour was removed. The left kidney did have an exceptional amount of work to do now to help recovery.

I made a conscious effort to drink lots of water and when my full English breakfast arrived that morning I was in heaven. Later that morning I got up and sat in the chair next to the bed. I managed to stand for a while too, although my legs weren't quite ready for a walk yet.

There was a world championship MotoGP (motorcycle) race on and we decked the room out with Valentino Rossi flags while we watched the race. We are big fans of MotoGP and Valentino Rossi is a god, or a 'g.o.a.t.' as some call him. Getting back to normality was now my goal; as normal as possible. Hazel coined the phrase 'new normal', and never was a truer word spoken.

My mum, Sister Karen and niece Ciara came to visit that morning and I had a few other visitors later in the day including my Uncle Jacky and Aunt Gill who were over from America. The regular tests continued, checking my statistics. All in all, though, I felt good, considering it was only day two.

Day three was a very different story.

I'd had a reasonable night. I was woken up every two hours for tests, but still felt rested and well and when Hazel arrived in the morning it all seemed good. I'd been out of bed the day before and now I had some more feeling back in my legs (the epidural was still in but reduced) so I asked the nurses if I could go for a walk.

My aunt Chloe had come to visit and was there along with Hazel when I left my room for a walk to the nurse's station, probably about twenty metres away. One of the nurses held my arm. The walk was very difficult as I had the stand with the drips and Louis Vuitton bag, etc. dangling from it, which we had to take with us. I was extremely unsteady on my feet and it was a struggle both mentally and physically. The return walk took ages and for the first time I felt totally beaten up.

I returned to the room, not euphoric as I'd expected, but in a state of utter despair. All of a sudden, and with the biggest of bangs, the gravity of the situation hit me and I broke down in uncontrollable tears. I felt alone, confused, helpless and frightened. I had never in my life been presented with something like this. I am a bit of a control freak and this was way out of my control. It was like somebody else had stolen my body and my mind — and I was not in a good place at all.

I didn't understand what had come over me. I was in no more pain and up until that point I had been doing well. For the first time really, my world and the thought that I could conquer it were falling apart.

My aunt left and even though the tears had subsided I was mentally confused, annoyed and frustrated. I was starting to understand that recovery was going to be more long term than I'd anticipated, and much more difficult. What was worse, I realised that I wasn't Superman after all. That was a bitter blow.

I fell into a deep slumber, Hazel by my side as ever. I was physically exhausted without a doubt, but mentally I was shattered too. I'd never felt like this at any time in my life before. What I didn't know was that while I was asleep, things got a little worse. Hazel told me later that after I'd been sleeping for a while the nurse came to do my regular stats, but couldn't wake me. Hazel had been creeping around the room quietly so as not to disturb me. Little did she know I was in more than a normal sleep: this was a coma.

All I can tell you is that when I did wake up there was a lot of fuss and a lot of people around me — a team of doctors and nurses that I didn't recognise. My temperature was over 40°C, my oxygen saturation was very low, breathing was laboured and my heart was racing. I remember opening my eyes and seeing all these people. I was confused and concerned. I didn't know immediately where I was or what was going on.

The lung infection was being treated by intravenous antibiotics after the operation and it seems as though it was getting worse instead of better. The epidural in my back had pulled out a bit too, so I was in much more pain than my body was able to cope with. They cooled me down with wet towels and fans. They put me back on one hundred per cent oxygen, painkillers, upped the level of antibiotics, and I was rushed off for an emergency chest X-ray and ECG.

Both the ECG and X-rays came back with no indication there was anything wrong, apart from the existing lung infection. I was feeling OK again, if a little miffed by the turn of events. One thing that did make me laugh at the time, and makes me smile even now, was the head of cardiology who looked over my ECG report.

I don't remember the cardiologist's name, but I asked him if I could take a look at the ECG printout and he asked me if I understood it. I said that I did, sort of. I took a quick look and returned it to him, suggesting that it looked fine. He took another long look at it and said it looked "pretty", which made me smile. I asked him if 'pretty' was a medical term, which in turn made *him* smile.

I was now being monitored more and I was accepting that the road to the 'new normal' might take a while. I needed to have a good talk to myself. This wasn't how it was going to be: I was going to make the decisions and I was in charge!

That evening I slept like a baby, albeit with regular two-hourly check-ups.

Day four and the world was indeed a very different place again. I'd had a chat with myself overnight and the world was round and spinning correctly once more. I asked for the epidural to be removed as it was uncomfortable now and having less and less effect. It also meant that there would be less on the stand to carry about with me when I wanted to go for another walk. And walk I did.

I felt like a new me. All my stats were good again. I walked twice the distance in half the time in the morning, and repeated it again in the afternoon with Hazel, much to the surprise of my visitors, Coz and Nok, who were over from Australia and had popped in to see me, as did some local friend Barry. All of the visits were short but I really appreciated the efforts they had made in coming to see me.

This was a top day. I felt so much better. Looking back, day three seems even more of a mystery. I spoke to Neil and the other doctors about it and they had no real explanation for the events of that day. It was just one of those things.

Day five was a very good day indeed. They removed the urinary catheter early, and later in the morning Hazel and I went for a walk out of the hospital and around the grounds. I was to see the doctors later in the day to see if I was allowed to go home.
I had more visitors and relished the fact I could show off how 'well' I was to my mates Eddy, Adrian and Tony.

Epidural out, Louis Vuitton bag gone, catheter gone and IV drips gone. I was looking good. I had a shave and a shower, I proved to the mobility nurse that I could walk up and down some test stairs, all I had to do was get my bowels to move (which they did with a little help from a couple of suppositories) and prove to the doctors I was well enough to go home. They were impressed with my recovery, especially after that little hiccup on day three, and the decision was made. They packed me off with a bucket load of drugs and their best wishes.

I would like to thank the staff at Frimley Park Hospital for all their help and support. They were brilliant.

Hazel drove us home, very carefully, and I was overjoyed to get back into our little house.

Now the big recovery started — at home.

Chapter Eight

Back home

I would like to say that being back home was the best thing in the world and in many ways, it was. However, in reality I wasn't very mobile, I was in pain and my body systems were still all over the place.

Hazel took two months off work as we'd expected me to be even more invalid than I was. I knew there would have to be some lifestyle changes generally and to my diet, which wasn't too bad but would have to improve. I had a single kidney now and I had to look after it. I didn't want any further complications and I certainly didn't want to end up on a dialysis machine. I didn't expect to be bedridden exactly, but I was in hindsight I was much better than we'd anticipated.

I slept when I needed to, I ate healthily and drank loads of water. However, there was one very strange thing going on that lasted for a while. I had very vivid, colourful dreams, usually bad ones. I had difficulty some days with the dreams versus reality. One night I got up to see if my eldest stepson Jack, was OK as I'd just had a shocker of a dream about him and I just could not convince myself that it wasn't real. I guess it was because of all the drugs and the fact that my body was having to do a lot of repair work and adjust to a new one-kidney regime.

Despite having been told in no uncertain terms to take it easy — hey, we always think we know best. Unfortunately, we *don't*. I tried to do too much too soon, and at times it was detrimental to my recovery. Too many people visited me on day one at home. I had cousins over from America and Australia and they all arrived together. It was too much really, I wasn't comfortable. They meant well and I was pleased see them, but in truth I was also pleased to see them all leave. After they left I just crashed, into the deepest of sleeps — a place I was to visit a lot during the following weeks. Every time I fell asleep I returned to the lurid world of my violent dreams. I hated it and I'm really pleased all that is well behind me.

I was single-minded in my determination about getting better and getting back to normal. However, as I discovered on day three in the hospital, it wasn't going to be easy and it was going to take time.

I started to write a daily diary, noting the events of the day, how I felt, drug usage and anything else that seemed relevant. After I started chemo I took down blood pressure, oxygen saturation, pulse rate and temperature — pretty much the same as the hospital had been doing. I knew I would have to slow down if I wanted to get better. Each day I was indeed feeling an improvement.

On the third day of being back at home we both hit a wall. Hazel and I were both shot. Was it a comedown? A relief? The worry? Bloody hell, I don't know — so many mixed emotions and repair work to do as well. We did absolutely nothing. We turned off the phone and pulled down the shutters that day, which turned out to be the best plan.

One thing that recovered quickly was my bowels. Nothing special, but after being constipated badly in hospital and needing suppositories to help achieve some movement, after just a couple of days at home I was back to my usual routine in that department.

After a week we returned to the hospital to see Neil Barber for a check-up. Here's my diary from the first few days at home...

Day 1... Dark day from the beginning. Too many people turned up at the same time — it is too much. I appreciate them coming but I'm pleased to see them leave us alone. Drugs for today were antibiotics and a mixture of paracetamol and ibuprofen.

Day 2... Couldn't be more different to day one — good night's sleep, bowels sorted and feeling positive again.
Drugs: Antibiotics and even though I took paracetamol and ibuprofen — it's less today, I feel more comfortable.

Day 3... Strange night's sleep or lack of it — though I feel fine. Hazel seems to have hit the wall. We are going to take it easy today. The day's been made up of sleeping, sleeping and some sleeping for dessert. I think we've made up for last night — the drug regime continues.

Day 4... Same sleep as the night before but I feel fine — so that's OK. Had a 50/50 morning great afternoon and evening. I have to be careful bending over as I hurt myself a bit yesterday bending over.

Chapter Nine

Check-up and a plan

Neil Barber came out of his office to call us in and was genuinely surprised by my health and demeanour. "Look at you!" he said and we all smiled broadly. I had a lot of questions about the operation, which he answered totally. We went through the pathology report on the tumour, which was now back from the labs.

As things turned out, I was lucky. The cancer was a known cancer and the front line drugs they use for the treatment of the secondary cancers are effective. In the past, traditional chemo treatments for secondary kidney cancer had a very low success rate, no more than 5% and even with more traditional chemotherapy the survival rate was on 8-13%. With the new drugs the survival rate is above 80%. Kidney cancer is one of the most treatable as a primary cancer. On the flip side, it's been one of the most difficult to treat as a secondary cancer in the past.

The pathology report stated that my cancer was bigger than the original CT scan had suggested and was a clear cell carcinoma. The tumour weighed 1.44kg, measured 22cm high x 15cm wide and 10.5cm deep. The conclusion stated it was a grade 3 clear cell carcinoma; T3b, Nx, Mx.

To explain: T3b is a staging (ranges between 1-4) and explains how advanced the cancer is. T3 is where the cancer has spread through the outer covering of the kidney (the capsule), to a major vein, the adrenal gland or other tissues around the kidney. The "b" suggests the tumour is more than 7cm. Nx is lymph node size, and because I didn't have any removed they were not on the pathology report. In this case the "x" suggested they are not present.

In Mx, the M is the grading of the Metastases or secondary cancer movements and again, because my secondary cancers were not removed the "x" was used to suggest they were not present.

For a more in depth explanation of cancer grading, both the MacMillan Cancer Support site and Cancer Research UK are excellent.

All being said and done, the operation was a great success. The tumour had come away cleanly even though it had fused to my liver and had had to be prized away. The scar was repairing well and all three of us were pleased. So much so, Neil Barber felt that a month after the operation I would be ready for chemo. He referred me to Professor Hardev Pandha who would now take over and decide how we would treat the remaining eight kidney tumours in the lymph nodes and lungs.

I asked how long this would all take. Neil said he expected I would have to have chemo with three-monthly CT scans for the first two to three years, followed by six-monthly scans for two years, moving eventually to annual and bi-annual scans for nine years. He also told me that I would have to go for monthly blood tests as the chemo is very strong and some people don't tolerate the drugs and side effects very well.

Basically, I was to carry on the good work. As far as he was concerned, his job was now done and it was time to move on.

Not for the first time, there was a new challenge waiting in the wings and something else I had to learn about and understand. After all, I wanted to get back to broking again in a couple of months' time. He said he would arrange for me to meet Professor Pandha in another three weeks, which would be a month after the operation.

Chapter Ten

The New Normal

I discovered in hospital and at home that you can push yourself too far too quickly and it will not only hurt, but moreover it slows recovery time. I wanted to be well so I decided on a regime that was flexible and had direction — back to the new normal.

I've never been a sleeper, not even as a young child, so when I returned home I knew I would need to listen to my body and sleep when it told me to. When I first returned home I did sleep a lot. In the past, when I've been ill, I've known how bad I was by the amount of sleep I required. This time I needed to sleep a lot. So, afternoon naps became usual and I slept anytime I felt the need.

It was strange because I would feel that the 'tank' was empty at times and I had to stop anything I was doing and sleep. Not just sleep, but 'die' into the deepest of sleeps. I can't remember ever sleeping so deeply and so much. I considered it to be repair time so I gave in.

When we had been planning my homecoming, Hazel and I both assumed I would be bedridden. Not totally invalid, but in bed more than out. Nothing could have been further from the truth.

Hazel took a couple of months off work to look after me, which I really appreciated. She kept an eye on me and stopped me doing anything too much, but in the right proportions, and sometimes encouraged me to do more. I wasn't allowed to drive the car for six weeks or ride my motorcycle for eight weeks as the scar, muscles and nerves had to recover. To this day, the nerves are still not as they were before; I have a 'dead patch' below the scar. Amusingly, a friend who had just seen my scar asked if the surgeon had put his whole head inside me. He said it looked like I'd been cut in half. An exaggeration of course — I'd only been cut in a quarter!

Every day I would get up and have breakfast, shave and shower and decide on the day. Sometimes Hazel would take me for a short drive to see people or we would just go for a drive, just to get out. I really enjoyed these trips out as the drive wasn't painful at all and I was able to physically prove to people I was getting better. It meant a lot to me.

You've read a few pages now and, hopefully, you can see my mental attitude throughout. However, one thing has never changed: the emotions.

I was and remain determined to be 'well'. I've often said to people I'm the healthiest ill person in the world. In my mind, especially after the operation, I felt that if we went to see people they could see that I was OK and getting better. It's a dilemma, of course. On one hand, I was indeed getting better from the operation. On the other hand, I still had eight tumours growing inside me. That was something to sort out in the future. Recovering from the operation and getting strong enough to start the next phase was my single minded goal at that point.

When I met people they would ask how I was. The standard answer was: "I'm fine, really good." Taking all things into consideration, I *was* doing well. After that, I would have to reiterate that I was indeed well. In many cases they would question if I really could have been that good; no one seemed to believe that I could really be that well.

I have said many times to people in the past, and still do, that if I could hard-wire you into my head, you would see that I'm in a good place. No pain, not frightened, and looking forward to getting back to the new normal. It was difficult to mask the fact that I still had eight cancerous tumours and I never hid from that myself, nor did I hide that from anybody else. I always told the truth about my condition, which may have upset a few people. But I've always felt that the truth was the best thing.

We all see the world from a different point of view. So my 'no pain', 'not frightened' and 'looking forward to getting back to normal' are not and can't be anybody else's map of the world. As such, I can only tell people the truth as I see, hear and feel it. They will draw their own conclusions.

I learned that a little adventure out of the house, even a short one, could take its toll. The next day it would take a long time to refill the tank. So I couldn't plan anything two days on the trot. I learned this early on and plans were made to adhere to always having a day of rest.

It was strange at home in one respect: I felt like a kid bunking off school at times. Yes, I was ill, but I'd never taken time off for a 'sickie'. I'd only been off work when I'd been genuinely ill and this did feel strange.

A long time before I was diagnosed, I had a chest infection. I coughed all the time, a dry cough that the usual over-the-counter drugs suppressed for a while. In hindsight, I should have gone to the doctor but, because it was more annoying than a problem, I didn't. While I was in hospital I had IV antibiotics and when I left, they gave me another course of antibiotics and a bucket load of pain killers.

I will talk more about my chest infection later on in the book, as something became blatantly obvious later on.

Here's an extract from my diary day on five...

"Good day – 8/10 I would say. Slept for six hours and only needed one Paracetomol in the morning and evening. I have one more day on antibiotics but the wheeze seems to be coming back which is a bit of a concern. I'm going to try and exercise more and expand my lung use.

"We went around to Mum's and my cousin popped in as he was over from Oz and was using my car while he was here."

After six days, Hazel and I decided that a short walk every day would help and, after taking advice, we started walking. I was able to walk more than two miles a day straight away, although I was often tired afterwards and needed a nap. I enjoyed the walks, they got me out of the house — even though the house was very much my happy place, always has been and still is.

Here's a funny thing. As I've already said, most days I would be up all day with the help of a nap or two. If I was having a bad day or needed more of a rest I would go back to bed. Bed became a sort of second home, my recovery pod if I'd pushed myself too far.

Day seven was Ciara's 18th birthday and she was having a gathering at The Three Pigeons in Guildford. I was a hundred per cent determined to be there and have a drink with her to celebrate. Hazel and I talked it over, and after the previous day's ground breaking walk I felt I could do it. I took the day very easy.

Karen my sister, Ciara, Richard her dad and Richard's girlfriend were there along with a few of their friends. I was very excited. I was going out in the evening, whooo hoooo!! We drove into town and parked outside the pub. I was so pleased to see everybody, even though I found it extremely emotional. In fact, as I write this, I am getting emotional again...

Here's a note from the diary — day 7, Ciara's birthday 27th June...

"Ciara is 18 today — Yahoo!!

"Antibiotics finish today, I had just 1 Paracetomol last night at bedtime. Slept 4 hours then 5 hours.

"Mum, Karen, Auntie Jill and Uncle Jacky popped in for a coffee as did Mark and Jane.

"All a bit too much I think. I had to shut down for a while in the afternoon."

Drinks for Ciara's 18th

As you can see from the photo, I looked OK. I'd lost ten kilos in weight so I looked drawn, but that evening I was super pleased with the world. This was just two weeks from the two operations.

We stayed for one drink, which took a while to drink. I had one pint of Guinness, a record small amount for me, and we went home. I think we both slept like babies that night. I felt I had set a goal of getting to Ciara's drinks, albeit for a short time, and I'd achieved it. That's what I've done ever since and, as I've got better and things have got easier, the goals have been set less consciously. I guess that is all part of getting life back to normal.

The other good thing was that after a week I needed less and less painkillers. I had enough to take down a large elephant if necessary, but already I was getting by with taking very few.

One thing I did suffer from was trying to doing something physical and then remembering that I had an eleven-inch scar. It was healing really well, but it was sore. I wasn't meant to lift anything or turn too far or too quickly. Whoops — I did forget a few times and afterwards I had to dig the painkillers out again. Oh well, lesson learned.

Chapter Eleven

The next challenge: Chemotherapy

At this point, I could get very technical because the world of oncology is like that, but I'm not going to. I want you to understand things from *my* point of view. Like most people with cancer, I don't know all the long complicated words and procedures. So, I made it clear to all the medical staff involved that I would appreciate simple terms. When and if I wanted more detailed information, I would ask for it.

It was back to the good old internet now as I now wanted to know everything I possibly could about chemotherapy. I not only researched online, I purchased several books, which I read like a starving man eats.

'Chemotherapy' is a generic term for various cancer treatments and has been the mainstay of cancer treatment for many years. I will do my best to give you a simple analogy for traditional chemotherapy treatment.

Chemotherapy is a type of cancer treatment using medicine to kill cancer cells. It does this by damaging or killing the cancer cells, so they can't reproduce and spread.

Imagine you have two sets of cells, one set normal and one set cancerous. You blast the cells with chemotherapy and both sets of cells are affected. The plan is that the normal cells recover and you leave the cancer cells weakened. The second treatment replicates the first but, with the cancer cells weaker, they have no time to recover and are again further killed off. The subsequent treatments will further kill the cancer cells, allowing the normal cells to recover. The problem has always been the collateral damage and the side effects this causes. Sometimes the normal healthy cells don't fully recover, leaving the patient with supplementary problems.

That is traditional chemotherapy, but I'm not on that. I'm on a targeted 'chemo' called a tyrosine kinase inhibitor (TKI). My drugs stop the cancer cells from creating proteins and a blood supply and as such, they can't survive and they die.

This goes some way to explaining the statistics I gave you earlier: traditional chemo for secondary kidney cancer had less than a five per cent survival rate and even with the Interferon chemotherapy it was only an eight to thirteen per cent chance of success. By comparison, my drug has a success rate in the region of eighty per cent plus — and I'll take those odds any day. There are now a bunch of front line drugs like mine being used in the battle against cancer.

But things are changing quickly. Towards the end of the book I will explain the new treatments and the old diseases i.e. genetically modified virus's working with your own brilliant immune system.

Chapter Twelve

Professor Hardev Pandha

Neil Barber referred me to the Nuffield Hospital Guildford to see Professor Hardev Pandha.

Professor Pandha is a consultant medical Oncologist at the Royal Surrey County Hospital, specialising in urological cancers including prostate and renal cancer. In addition to his work in the NHS he is also Head of Urological Oncology at the University of Surrey, managing a research group which is investigating novel biomarkers and targeted therapies for cancer. If I was going to be referred to anybody, he was the right man.

An appointment was made and I must say, I was very nervous about this meeting. The reality was that after the operation and a month of good recovery we had a big battle ahead dealing with the remaining eight 'aliens'. Yet again, I didn't know what to expect. I'd seen friends and family on chemotherapy, and it's not pretty. I had a lot to learn and it all seemed daunting and confusing.

Neil Barber said something very valuable to me while I was in hospital which I would like to pass on. He said that I had a team around me. He was part of the medical team as were his colleagues and the staff at Frimley Park Hospital. He also said that family and friends were a very important part of my team. Now I was moving on to the next phase and I would have a new team around me; Professor Pandha and his staff would be taking over from where Neil had left off.

I'm sure I will mention this more than once in this book but my 'team' have been and continue to be very special to me. They are everything: my support, my motivation, my shoulder to cry on, my counsel and very much my safety net. They give me a will to live and a future. I want to be around for a long time and often they don't realise how much I appreciate their love and support. They are my strength.

Hazel and I met Professor Pandha at the Nuffield and we reviewed the situation as it was, and what we were going to do about it. I'm pleased to say, and not for the first time, that we met with a very professional and approachable member of the medical fraternity. There were no questions then or now, simple or complicated (well, complicated in *my* world) that were not answered in full.

The Prof, as he's affectionately known, has an arsenal of drugs that can be used these days and, as far as I could see, it was going to be a case of suck it and see to start with. If drug 'A' didn't work, we would give drug 'B' a go, and so on.

A plan was set and I was going to be taking a daily amount of a tyrosine kinase inhibitor called Pazopanib. I would have to have a monthly blood test as these drugs are powerful and they have to monitor how well your body copes with them. The drugs are only issued after the blood test has been reviewed by the Prof or one of his registrars. I would also have to have CT scans every three months to see if the drugs were having the desired effect on the remaining tumours and to make sure that the cancer cells running around my body hadn't 'picked' in or had tried to grow anywhere else in my body.

It was a lot to take in and think about. I still had cancer, in actual fact eight cancers, and the CT scan showed that I also had a mark on my pelvis that indicated the cancer had tried to pick in there as well.

We knew the enemy and we had a plan. All we had to do was start and, as bizarre as it might sound, I couldn't wait to get stuck in. It was the same with the operations: I knew that the sooner I started, the sooner I would be fixed. Again, I wanted to get on with getting better.

The meeting with Professor Pandha was informative, interesting and he was very supportive. I was given some telephone numbers I could call twenty-four hours a day for help and assistance. Would I like to speak to a counsellor or dietitian? I didn't feel I needed either but I appreciated the offer. There is a lot of support for cancer sufferers, something a lot of patients don't realise.

At the time I didn't know it, but that meeting with Professor Pandha would have an ongoing influence on my life, as you will find out later in the book.

After a forty-minute consultation I returned to the waiting room and sat while the pharmacist brought me my drugs. The pharmacist didn't just give me the drugs but sat me down and specifically explained the regime, which I found surprising. However, these are no over-the-counter drugs and need to be treated with respect and understanding.

Pretty much all the drugs I'd needed to take in the past had been taken with food and definitely not on an empty stomach. The drugs I was to take now had their own regime. They couldn't be taken any less than two hours before eating and one hour after eating, i.e. on a very empty stomach. There were a few other warnings: no grapefruit or grapefruit juice and no supplements. I was warned in no uncertain terms that all I needed was a healthy balanced diet. Plenty of fresh fruit, vegetables and buckets of water. I had to remember that I only had one kidney now and had to look after it. Although, that's not a biggie really, as many people live with only one kidney.

The next shock to the system was the list of possible side effects. Wow, I'd never seen so many!

I collected my drugs and went home. I couldn't take them that day as I'd already planned dinner and effectively there wasn't a three-hour window in which to take them. I rearranged my routine and started taking them the next day.

I was excited about taking the drugs in a way, as I was confident they would work. So the drugs became part of my 'team' as well. The only problem was, the drugs were like a naughty child and would have a whole world of challenges for me.

Chapter Thirteen

Pazopanib and advice

The drug of choice was Pazopanib, which is a front line tyrosine-kinase inhibitor, one of many, but the one that the Prof thought would work well with me. He has vast experience in this so I was more than happy to take his suggestion. To be honest, this was another moment when I felt a little helpless as there are many drugs, all with long complicated names and, as a patient, you really don't have a clue. I put my faith in the new team members and on day one I popped in two 400mg pills which were to be my life as far as we could see, forever. There's no plan to stop at this point.

These drugs are targeted drugs and nothing like the traditional chemotherapy. I take pills every day, nothing intravenous. Moreover, they are specific to *my type* of kidney cancer. That said, they have subsequently found that these sort of targeted drugs do have applications on other cancers in other areas.

I was offered an endless amount of advice from various people about alternative medicines. Some made a bit of sense, some were outlandishly stupid. Almost all had no definitive studies done and were only supported by anecdotal evidence. No great shock as often these 'miracle' cures meant buying products (some illegal), most online and at great cost. If you think the alternative path is your way then that is, of course, up to you. However, everyone should carefully consider the path they take — after all, you can't buy time back. I hate the thought that some of these so called 'cures' are taking advantage of some very vulnerable people.

The 'alternative' regime was never a consideration for me. One of my heroes, Barry Sheene, died after following an alternative cancer regime, as have a couple of my friends. Would they still be with us if they had stuck to the tried, tested and more importantly, highly researched medical treatments?

Whenever I was offered any advice, I faithfully wrote everything down and asked the Prof about it. He explained them, and dismissed them generally, with a warning that even something as innocent as vitamin C could have a detrimental effect on the Pazopanib. These types of drugs are relatively new and, as such, little research has been done on the effect of supplements on the drugs. After all, why would you waste money on researching vitamin supplements when for the most part, they are passed through the body with no effect because you don't need them. You can get all your dietary needs from a healthy diet with fresh fruit and vegetables.
As I've said, I kept a daily diary upon my return home. I added blood pressure, heart rate, oxygen saturation and temperature. It is difficult sometimes to read back as there were some very dark days, but they got better and it's been an invaluable reference for writing this account.

I started taking my drugs faithfully the next day, and the next and the next. I was starting to think that all the side effects I had read and been advised about were not going to apply to me. Oh dear, oh dear…

Here's an extract from the 15th July 2013, the first day on Pazopanib…

"BP 117/81, Heart rate 80 bpm, temp 36.3c, oxygen saturation 98%.
Today starts phase 2 — chemo starts tonight. 2 x 400mg of Pazopanib once a day.
I collected the pills from the hospital and popped around to mum's. I managed to do a good amount of jobs. Feeling good — Pazopanib will help me kill the cancers."

The list of side effects is extensive and I was advised by both the Prof and the pharmacist that many, some or all might apply. Add to this the fact that they were likely to change over time, and it was clearly going to be a balancing act. Long medical names, side effects I'd never heard of and yet more long medical names of drugs — I was going to have to cope with the side effects. My mind was, as you would expect, in a tizz!

As I've previously said, everyone who has cancer has their own personal cancer. It becomes more evident as you start the treatment that the published side effects could, would, might or might not affect you. Did I care? Not at all as I had eight mini-aliens living and growing inside me and I needed to do something about them. I was feeling positive, and with my new chum Pazopanib, we were up for the fight.

I'm not going to list all the possible side effects, just the ones that affected me. On day four of the pills the side effects started. Oh boy, did they start!

Chapter Fourteen

Side effects

I always kept at the front of my mind that, regardless of side effects, the end result was that I was going to live longer and as much as possible lead a normal life. The 'new normal' as Hazel said.

You read a lot about cancer sufferers and their side effects. The most common sight is that of bald women and children on traditional chemotherapy. Some of the chemo treatments do cause hair loss, which didn't worry me as I'd been bald for years. My treatment didn't cause this at all — in fact, it's had the opposite effect, as I will explain.

Day three on the drugs was 18th July, my birthday, and so far so good. I had a really good birthday, mostly because of my wonderful wife. I had noted that for the first time my blood pressure was elevated at 141/93.

Here's an extract from the diary on my birthday...

"Brilliant 54th birthday – mostly due to my brilliant wife! Lunch at the Mulberry Inn, Chiddingfold and popped into mum's. Still feeling fine — BP up a tad — keeping tabs on all."

However, on the fourth day the side effects really started. I had a shocking night's sleep and woke up with a bad headache. I don't get headaches generally and this one was particularly horrible. I got up feeling drained and started taking my daily stats. Hmmm, blood pressure through the night was 146/104 but by early in the morning (4:15am) it had settled a tad to 144/96. I spoke to the hospital and they suggested some over-the-counter drugs to get rid of the headache and to lower the BP.

As you will see, a day later there was a noticeable change as this is another extract from my diary...

"Bad headache overnight. Blood pressure (BP) 146/104 settled to 146/98 by 04:15. Heart rate 67 beats per minute (BPM) and 97% oxygen saturation. Talked to the Nuffield (hospital). Took 1gm of Paracetomol & 400mg of Ibuprofen. Headache later gone.
Strange day — a few side effects for the first time. Metal taste, hands felt pumped up, BP up — tired all day. Good to see Hannah and Luke (niece and her boyfriend) — felt OK by 7pm."

I also noticed a few other changes. My hands and arms felt pumped up, probably due to the blood pressure, and I had a bizarre metallic taste in my mouth all the time. The fish and chips we had that evening were the last things I tasted for almost a year as my taste buds went and everything from then on was like eating cardboard tinged with a metallic taste.

All of a sudden, I who love my food had no interest in it. It wasn't repulsive, there was just no taste to it at all, only different textures. Even my favourite food in the world, Japanese, was taste free. The only thing I could in any way enjoy was something sweet.

But I knew I had to eat and I knew I had to eat well in order to be as healthy as possible. So, regardless of the boring monotony of metallic tasting cardboard, I ate well, drank loads of water and dreamed of food tastes in the past.

To add to my woes, I couldn't use normal toothpaste anymore, because it was too strong, and I had to use the most sensitive that I could find. Normal mouthwash positively burned my mouth, or so it felt. I switched to Diflam as a mouthwash, having been recommended by the oncology nurse, and it was very good.

As much as I was concerned about my raised blood pressure, it is an expected side effect of the Pazopanib, so I went to see my GP. I was put on a low dose of an ACE inhibitor (with opens the blood vessels, unlike a 'beta blocker' which thins the blood). It worked straight away but I did struggle with the first drug called Amlodipine (5mg daily); at the time I thought that the drug was causing other side effects or escalating existing side effects.

Looking back at drug effects and wellbeing in the first six months, I realise there were some errors made and I that should have stuck with some of the original drugs. I now know that it wasn't necessarily the drugs I was taking to help cope with the side effects being problematic, it was the very powerful Pazopanib which was the cause. There have been a few foods I've also stopped eating in the hope of reducing the side effects — to no avail. Live and learn, Kim, live and learn!

In the early days I went to my local GP a lot. We adjusted doses, changed drugs and investigated worries that I had. We worked on getting a regime that gave me quality of life and as much freedom as possible. I changed the blood pressure drug and started on a low dose of Ramipril 2.5mg daily which I'm still on today and very happy with. My blood pressure was more constant when I checked it daily. And, even though I don't do such regimented checks these days, my blood pressure remains very controlled.

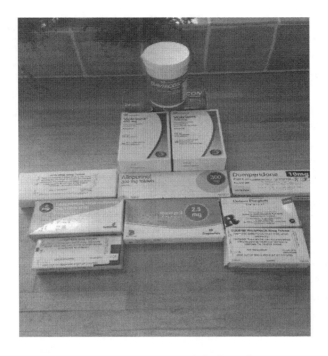

These are the drugs I needed early on

I'm sure there are many cancer patients like me, who deal with side effects as they come up. The problem is, you never know what is going to affect you. We all get lists of potential side effects but, because cancer is such a personal thing and very much a moving target, you never know what's coming next or what to do. Then it changes again.

The medical system in this country is fantastic. There's never been a question I've asked that's not been answered. I've requested all my reports, results and CT scans and they've been produced without question, although I do have to pay to get a CD copy of my CT scans from the NHS.

After a couple of months on Pazopanib the hair all over my body had turned polar white and I hated it. I'd had a goatee beard before the operation and after I started the chemo, but I hated it going white so I shaved it off. I decided eventually to regrow it and today I have a neat white goatee. It is now an established thing and hopefully makes me look a little more distinguished.

As the scar started to heal I decided to go swimming, which is a great overall regime for exercising. We are lucky to have a fantastic Olympic-sized pool a couple of miles away at the Surrey Sports Park. It has a common changing area and as I was getting changed I became very aware of the large scar across my right side. I must say, it did bring a wry smile to my face.

My wry smile changed to open laughter as I encountered a group of schoolgirls leaving the pool to get changed. The first of the girls saw the scar on the portly white-haired man and giggled with her friends. Then the rest of the group saw what they were looking at as I walked past them. I politely said hello to their teacher, who was a little mystified herself, until she saw the scar. Oh well, no harm done and it did amuse me.

I dived into the pool which I found refreshing, and proceeded to swim a kilometre. I honestly felt I could have done more but, for a first swim, albeit a slow one, it was enough. I'd lost almost 10kg in weight and my eyebrows and eye lashes were as white as fresh snow.

One thing that really did upset me in the early days were photos of me. It may sound ridiculous to you but I hardly recognised myself in photos and I hated it — really hated it!
I had a new struggle as my 'look' concerned me. I've never been the best looking bloke around and I'm certainly not vain, but this dramatic change was too much at times. I also looked very pale all the time. I had no hair colour (is polar white a colour?!), my face was pale and I was gaunt (in comparison to normal). It really upset me and even now, after almost two years on the drugs, I still don't like those early post-operative photographs of me.

The other thing about my hair was its length. Hair seems to be a pretty self-regulating length, apart from facial and head hair. Now, I found I had outrageously long hair all over the place. One of the hairs under my arm we measured (before trimming it) at eight inches!

Through all the dark stuff there's been a lighter side to all this and we've always tried to have a laugh. Here's a quick story that's always amused us.

I was lying in bed at night with Hazel after showering. I looking down at my white body and I pulled up my pubic hair, which was somewhat longer than it used to be. I mused that it looked like Don King's hair (a famous American boxing promoter). If you don't know what he looks like it is worth Googling him; he has mad hair! We cried laughing and still smile widely at it today. All very silly.

My issues with my new look were of course psychological. I was still very much the person I'd always been and, as I was finding out, much stronger than I had ever realised. I just had to get to terms with it as there were bigger problems to deal with; the physical adjustment to the Pazopanib.

The next problem was about to emerge and it really was me being bloody-minded that caused it.

I'd been warned about 'hand/foot' syndrome, which can cause sensitive skin and blistering.

I was due to go to the hospital and it was a lovely day so I decided to walk there and back, a three mile round trip. The distance was fine as I'd been walking that far on a regular basis. It was a lovely day, but not too sunny. My skin had become very sensitive to too much sunlight, so I covered up just in case. I was at least being sensible in *that* department.

The walk was fine, no worries, and later in the day I went shopping with my mother and sister.

We went to Costco and walked around for a long time. I was on my feet all the time and my feet now felt sore.

At this point I should have rested and kept off my feet. However, the following day I went to the car auctions with my cousin Stephen and his son David. They do a great breakfast at the auctions, which was sadly lost on me to be honest, as there was no real taste. While we were there, and pretty much all day, my feet were really sore; so much so, I was standing on the side of them at times.

I got home and was so glad to get off my feet. I had overdone it, of course. My feet were a mess and had blistered all over. Dry, massive blisters covered both my feet and they were very painful. That was it for four days. I was back in bed and had to crawl around the house on my hands and knees just to get to the bathroom. It was ridiculous. I'd been very stupid and not listened to my body warnings. Boy, did I pay the price! My feet were so painful and, because I was going everywhere on my hands and knees, they were also sore. Time to drag the painkillers out again.

When I regained some mobility I arranged an additional meeting with Professor Pandha and his specialist nurses and they were surprised. Pazopanib doesn't commonly cause hand/foot syndrome that bad, which makes me rare. It was decided that I should come off the Pazopanib and give my feet and skin a chance to recover, and everything else time to settle.

I had a week off the drugs, which did concern me. I was worried that coming off the drugs would cause them to lose their effect. Those worries were soon put to bed by the ever-supportive Prof.

My feet settled down quite quickly. I saw a chiropodist, who made me some pads and gave me great advice. The very best thing was the cream that the Prof recommended for my feet: 'Udderly Cream', which was created to treat cows' udders! Well, it turns out to be good for cancer treatment side effects too. Fantastic then, fantastic now. Even today I have to be careful with my skin as it's very sensitive.

I've learned over time about what shoes to wear and how to look after my feet and skin. I think that will be ongoing for as long as I'm on the drug. I do have shoes that are more user friendly now, and insoles for others. I've learned to take it easy and to heed the warning signs.

Back on the drugs after the short break, the next side effect that was to become worse and worse as time went by was diarrhoea.

According to the side effects list, fifty per cent of people on the drug get diarrhoea and I was very much one of those. The control drug of choice was Loperamide, which is better known as the over-the-counter drug Imodium. I could take up to eight a day of the 2mg capsules.

Looking back, I realise I made a schoolboy error with my drugs in the early days. I wanted to take the least amount possible but the cost was in many cases a painful one. If I had taken the suggested dosages and not what I *thought* I could take as a minimum, I would have had a better quality of life and suffered the side effects less. Oh well, I was not issued with an instruction book for Kim's Cancer, so I had to learn on the job. The specialist nurse insisted that I took the drugs I needed to give me back some quality of life. In the early days I was very much of the opinion that the minimum drug intake was the best. That opinion remains, but I have learned to use the drugs in a way that better suits me and which has indeed given me back a better life quality.

I often underused the Loperamide and I had some rotten times with the diarrhoea. Luckily, I've never been incontinent, but having constant diarrhoea is not nice. The other thing was, the more I used the Loperamide, the more nausea I seemed to get. So another drug was needed to stop me feeling sick, Domperidone. It sounds like a good bottle of Champagne, but sadly is nothing like that.

Was the nausea caused by the use of Loperamide or the Pazopanib? I don't know, but I was advised to use Codeine as an alternative to Loperamide to address the diarrhoea and have managed with that far better ever since. I do get nausea from time to time but these days it doesn't stop me in my tracks as it did in the early days. I use Codeine and some Loperamide, or change it around to give myself a break from one for a while. This may not be a sound medical thing to do but it works for me — and as I've found, if it works it works.

I thought I had things pretty much under control, and seeing as my physical repair from the operation was very much on track, I was starting to think about a return to work and getting on with my life soon.

Chapter Fifteen

Getting into a regime

I was told from the start of the drug regime that I would have to go for regular blood tests and CT scans.

In the original consultation with Neil Barber, he suggested that for the first couple of years I would be going for a CT scan every three months. By year three it would be scans every four months, year four every six months, and after that annually for up to nine years. This, of course, would always be dependent on everything going to plan.

A nine year plan; now that's what I *call* a plan! However, as I've found out since, nothing is written in stone and flexibility is key to health and recovery. I've found that I have to adapt and change. Cancer is unique to the person with it.

When Hazel and I first met Professor Pandha, he explained what he considered to be the best path forward after reviewing my case and offered me several options. If the first suggested option didn't work or it wasn't as effective as we'd hoped, then there were always alternatives.

Kidney cancer is a very treatable cancer as a primary tumour, as long as the tumour comes away cleanly. Unfortunately, as a secondary cancer or metastatic cancer, it is one of the most difficult cancers to treat. The targeted drugs I take are life savers to say the least, and give kidney cancer sufferers like me tangible hope for the future. Life expectancy before these targeted drugs were developed was up to fifteen per cent (using the traditional chemotherapy). Now, with the targeted drugs it's more than eighty per cent!

This is a major step forward and with new immunotherapy treatments being trialled all the time the future for cancer sufferers is much brighter.

Professor Pandha explained the drug of choice, the good, the bad and the ugly of the drug and said I would have to have monthly blood tests and three to four monthly CT scans for as long as I was on the drug, in other words forever. The reality is that kidney cancer is difficult to scan. Only CT scans work and even then, all they can do is give the size of the tumour. A dye has not yet been discovered to enable to more accurate PET scans or MRI scans to be used. Work in progress I guess.

The targeted drugs are very powerful indeed and, as I found out, have various and variable side effects. More importantly, the doctors have to keep tabs on how your body is reacting to these drugs. In my case, they need to have a continual picture as to the condition of my remaining kidney, the adrenal gland (as I only have one now) and the rest of my organs and body.

Every month I go to St Luke's Oncology unit and have a blood test followed by a consultation with the Prof or one of his colleagues the next day. In our consultations, he reviews my blood tests and general health. We discuss any problems, I get weighed, my blood pressure is taken and if everything is okay, I get another thirty days of Pazopanib.

I'm pleased to say that my bloods have always been pretty good but from time to time there are anomalies. For instance, the thyroid shows to be out of line but experience tells the Prof that this is caused by the drug and that everything is actually fine with my thyroid function.

If at any time there is something we're not happy about, then further investigation is undertaken. Here's an example: I had an ongoing sore throat, very sore in fact. Every time I swallowed it was painful. I went to my local GP and I also spoke to the Prof. They both said it was most likely a virus and could take months to heal. Being a doctor myself (not!), I thought it might be the cocktail of drugs I was taking at the time. They both dismissed this.

After months and a course of antibiotics, my throat continued to be painful and it was now really worrying me. I was referred to an Ear, Nose and Throat specialist who decided to have a closer look at the throat and to see if it was anything more.

In the past, I'd never worried about an odd ache or pain, a cold, bruise or cut. You know, the sort of thing we get sort of all the time but never really pay much attention to. However, since I've had cancer, I still don't worry too much about the little aches and pains, but I have found that I have become more aware of them. Maybe because the sore throat hung around for so long, alarm bells started ringing in my head. I didn't think I had throat cancer or anything, but I had become hyper-aware of any problems.

We all get bio feedback from our bodies, most of which we chose to ignore, otherwise we would all be at the doctor all the time. Sometimes, we get continuous bio feedback that we shouldn't ignore and we *should* go to the doctor.

This brings me onto an important point. Did I notice the swelling under my ribs at any time before I went to the doctor? When I think back, as I've done plenty of times, I can't remember a time I noticed anything, at least, not consciously. When I did decide to go to see somebody, it wasn't a moment too soon. Nobody wants to waste the doctor's time but, in many cases, if we listened to our bodies more and took action, we would catch diseases more quickly while they are more treatable. This isn't just the case for cancer, but for many other maladies as well.

My father was a case in point. He never went to the doctor, or probably no more than six times in his whole life before he died at seventy-two. His hospital notes were only two pages long, and they covered his entire life. Should he have gone to the doctor? Yes, without a doubt! I'm sure he should have many times but he was very frightened and it just wasn't his way. He wasn't afraid of the doctors per se, but of what the doctor might tell him or find. This, I've discovered, is much more common than you might think.

There's one thing I should say: it's better to go along and find out what is wrong, than leave it until it's too late. You can't buy back time.

As for my father, he died of multiple cancers and we really only knew when he was admitted to hospital after his spine had collapsed and his kidneys were just about to give up.
He died nine days after admission and it must have taught me a subconscious lesson because, when I found that swelling, I went to see the doctors very quickly.

At the ENT specialist I explained the sore throat situation and he had a look down my gullet. He couldn't see anything apart from an obvious sore throat, but he decided to inspect further with the use of a camera. I can't say it was the most pleasant of experiences, to have a camera on a flexible tube pushed up my nose and down my throat. But it did give him a good chance to see what was going on. He concurred with the other doctors that it was just a sore throat —but said if it didn't clear he would scan me to make sure there was nothing more serious going on.

The throat didn't get any better so he sent me for a CT scan, which came back clear. One revelation was the fact I'd broken my nose at some time in the previous fifty-four years! I was obviously pleased about the results and I just had to wait for the sore throat to run its course. That course turned out to be eight months long.

Regular CT scans are easy: you turn up, get into a dressing gown, drink lots of water, lie down on the machine and they put a canula in your arm so the dye can be administered. You slide in and out of the machine and it gives you commands with regards to holding your breath and then breathing again. It's a big machine and looks like a giant Polo mint with a table through the middle of it.

Once you are lying on the table under the scanner, they insert a cannula in your arm and the dye is administered automatically. You are warned that the dye can give you some strange sensations and it does in my case. I'm sure these are different for everybody but I find I get a metallic taste in my mouth, warm feeling in my blood, almost like I've been attached to a central heating system, and the weirdest of all, I feel like my testicles are being tickled... All very strange.

I'm in the machine for less than ten minutes. The sensations abate quite quickly and I await the results. I've found that after some of the CT scans I feel very tired and have no energy. It could be either physical or mental, but let me explain.

As I've already said in this book, the emotional side of cancer is much worse than the physical for me. Every three months to start with, and now every four months, I go for a scan. I have to wait a week before I go to see the Prof for the results. I purchase a CD copy of the scan from the NHS for £10 so that when I get home I can have a look. The truth is, I can't really see anything apart from the major bits and bobs and I have come to really admire the radiologist's skills. Talk about fifty shades of grey!

When I go for my consultation it is an emotional roller coaster. I feel fine, but then again, I felt fine before I noticed the swelling under my ribs. And herein lies the head spin.

So far, all the results that I've had have been great. The six kidney tumours on my lungs have gone (as in they no longer present an image or trace on the CT scan) and the kidney tumours on the lymph nodes are greatly reduced- less than half the size in fact.

I'm over the moon about this and it strengthens my resolve, but every four months I know in the darkest corners of my mind that there could be another cancer. The cancer may have started to grow somewhere else. The existing tumours may have started to grow again. The drug may have stopped working. Who knows and that's the problem: nobody knows, it's a constantly moving target.

After one of my scans in particular I had a rare mental and emotional problem, when waiting for the results. I'm usually very strong and positive and definitely feel like I'm the boss, the cancer will have to do what I want to do. However, in this particular instance, in the days leading up to my consultation with the Prof, the 'worry chip' in my head went into overdrive.

I consider myself to have a very level view of life. I know I'm going to die, we all are. Realistically, we start to die from the minute we're born. We just don't know when or from what. This particular scan sent me into a head spin. I'd looked at the scan and couldn't see anything but I started to worry, and then I worried some more. Like all fears and phobias, this head spin took off and became all consuming.

The day before meeting the Prof for the results I was at home as I wasn't teaching, and I cried most of the day. I was scared, really scared, for the first time. I'm not scared of pain and I'm definitely not scared of dying. But I have too much to do yet and too many things to see and I'm not ready to die. I could not clear my head at all and when poor Hazel got home from work, I lost it properly.

I cried like a baby telling her I didn't want to die, I wasn't finished yet, there was more to do! There was a total outpouring of emotions. As ever, she was brilliant and eventually calmed me down. Tomorrow I was going to see the Prof and all would be revealed. This was my worst reaction by far to the CT scans, emotionally speaking. I've been much more circumspect ever since. The problem is that every time you get scanned they could indeed find a further problem. It's like the first consultation all over again but every three to four months.

What was the result? Good: all the tumours were smaller, cancer hadn't 'picked' in anywhere else and I was reacting very well to the treatment. Happy days!

Since then, I've always had a good talk to myself beforehand — after all, it will be whatever it will be and there's nothing much I can do, apart from eat well, drink plenty of water and keep that positive attitude.

This is yet another example of the emotions of cancer and I'm lucky, I have the best people around me with more love than any person can ask for. I can cry, laugh and fall, there's always someone there to catch me. I do have a deep sympathy for people who are going through this by themselves.

I've already mentioned information you can find on cancer but later in the book I will give you some more contacts for help and advice.

Chapter Sixteen

The return to work

Even though this chapter is about my return to work I would like to start by thanking the directors and staff at Tullett Prebon for their understanding and care.

The scar repair was going well and I was in pretty good physical shape generally, so it was time to get back to work. I wasn't allowed to drive my car for six weeks, but when I did it was fine. The restriction on the motorcycle was eight weeks and, again, when I did go out for a ride — it was fine. The car was easy and I'd been out in Hazel's car many times. The bike is much more physical so I had to be careful and when I first starting riding again, I did get tired. Maybe it was the excitement of being back on the bike — I do love riding the bikes!

So by the time I was ready for work, I was *really* ready for work — not only physically, but I had my beloved transport back as well. I thought the return to work was going to be seamless but it turned out to be less so.

I'd spoken to all my customers and colleagues pretty much since I'd been off and I'd been up to the office twice in my three months' absence. I contacted Human Resources at work and told them that as far as the medical and oncological teams were concerned, I was fit to return to work. It would be three months to the day that I had left and I was fit enough to ride the motorcycle up to the City of London and start my normal 6.00am trading.

On my return I did find it a little surreal. Nothing in essence had changed, the job was still the job and after all those years, I'd not forgotten what needed to be done. It did take quite a while though to sink in that I was back at work.

I wanted to get straight back into the swing of things, but first I had to see the company doctor. The meeting with him was interesting as I was prepared to go back to work five days a week, but he was thinking about two days only. He didn't understand the industry I worked in and even suggested that I work those two days a week from home. My job was in one of the very few 'open outcry' markets left and after explaining this, he conceded two days a week for at least the first month back.

Let me explain open outcry markets. Many of the financial market products are now transacted by computer. The most famous of these was the stock market which was open outcry but has succumbed to technology. You may have also seen men in brightly dressed jackets shouting orders at each other. Well, the market I worked in was similar to that, but without the silly jackets.

I really wasn't very happy about this new working arrangement as it seemed pointless. It wasn't fair on me, it wasn't fair on my customers and it wasn't fair on my colleagues either. While I was away my accounts had been covered by colleagues, but I wanted to get back into it and deal with my own accounts. There would be little continuity in this plan and I was upset as I felt he was being too cautious. He wasn't of course, he was doing the right thing and I was being bombastic. I did eventually win a slight concession and I was allowed to work three days a week for the first month (unless there were problems) and return for monthly consultations, of which there would be four more.

Truth be told, I'm sure my colleagues would have been happier if I'd never returned. Things had moved on and my colleagues were busily building relationships with my customers. Now I was back, it complicated things as it was only to be for three days a week. Thinking back with that marvellous thing called hindsight, I should have never gone back into that industry. It was all too much — but I had to give it a go, as I will explain.

From the moment I was diagnosed I had a plan. Well, there were two plans really. The medical one, which I had to adhere to as I can't operate on myself clearly, and then there was MY plan. My plan was to recover from the operation as soon as possible. Get out of hospital as soon as possible. Get back to work within three months. The medical plan was much more open ended, in as much as there wasn't a time frame and we would move forward when and if I was fit enough and well.

I needed goals, so I set them. Some were a little too ambitious and I paid the price, like walking too far or not sleeping enough, that sort of thing. The goals I set pushed me forward to the 'new' normal I wanted so much. I won't be defined by cancer. I didn't want people worrying about me and I didn't want any special concessions just because I'd had an operation and was fighting the remaining aliens. I must admit though, in my single minded approach to the whole thing I did worry other people as they thought that I was pushing too hard and too fast. OK, I put my hands up. In many cases they were right.

Work for me was different when I returned, for a couple of reasons.

Firstly, I had a regime of pills to take and the side effects to take care of. The worst and most constant and sometimes awkward was the diarrhoea. I can't say I suffered from fatigue, which is a common side effect. The blood pressure was well controlled even in the most stressful of times. The other side effects were not too bad.

Secondly, my enthusiasm for the job had waned. I honestly don't know whether it was my illness, the fact I'd been doing the job for so long, a combination of it all — or was it time just to draw a veil over the whole thing?

All that said, I was back. I was in pretty good physical shape. I continued the job as I always had and I was now, at last, working full time. In the last couple of months, life had been non-stop and there was little time to relax. There was a chance to take a holiday and after talking to the doctors — my own, the company doctor and the Prof — we all decided it was OK to go on holiday, which in this case meant to France skiing.

Chapter Seventeen

Time for a holiday!

I'd been back in the market since the September and I was getting to grips with my new life. I was looking forward to Christmas and the New Year, in fact, especially the New Year as we were booked to go skiing.

Of all the things that I love to do, skiing is up there along with scuba diving and riding motorcycles. We have been skiing almost every year since Hazel and I have been together. For the most part there was Hazel and myself, Jack and Nathan, Bryan, Lorraine and their two children, Hannah and Jacob.

We've been on plenty of holidays over the years as a group of eight, including skiing, visits to the South of France where Hazel's parents had a place, Portugal a couple of times and we've also all been scuba diving together in Turkey, Egypt and Cyprus. These have been some of my favourite holidays. I love spending time with them.

Before going for our week of skiing I spoke to the Prof and asked what the best regime would be. At that time, I was on a lot of drugs to counter the Pazopanib side effects and, looking back, I wasn't all that in control at times. He suggested that I took a week off the Pazopanib and the side effects would decrease quickly. I'd already had a short break when my feet were problematic so I had done it before — and it had worked.

I was still worried about this though, and said so. Especially after the initial and favourable CT scans, I didn't want to mess everything up. He said that in the big picture, seven days off the drug wouldn't make much difference as there would be a residual amount in my blood stream. In saying that, he did say to keep on the blood pressure pills.

This was the first time since July I'd had any sort of break from the drug and I was excited that I would hopefully be side effect free.

I did have concerns about going skiing. Diarrhoea had been the most consistent side effect. Skiing out on the French Alps might be 'interesting' bearing in mind French toilets and the general lack of them on the slopes. These days I have a good drug regime, but back then I will still playing with dosages and drugs and I didn't want to be caught short on a ski slope!

There was also a concern about getting tired and bringing on fatigue — it goes without saying that skiing is a physically demanding sport.

I've been lucky with fatigue in as much as I've not really suffered much from it at all. But when I do get tired, I shut down. The only comparison I can give you is if you've been on a long haul flight and you get jet lag — it's the same sort of thing. When you are tired, it doesn't matter what time of day or night it is, you have to stop and sleep.

Even though I was concerned about fatigue the bottom line was, if I needed to I could always stay in the chalet and rest whilst the others skied.

With all concerns packed away in my bag, off we went.

How was the skiing? Fantastic as ever. How was I? Very well indeed. Side effects? As I'd been advised, they abated. Diarrhoea was well controlled, as was everything else, and we had a great trip.

Skiing in Les Gets – Love it!

Like many of these things since the operation, it was very much about getting over a mental obstacle rather than a physical one. I felt a great sense of achievement and although my skiing was a little more 'sensible' than my usual standard, I loved it. This was a great break from (almost) everything.

I came back from the trip with some great photos and memories.

Chapter Eighteen

The final walk... or was it?

On my return from holiday I realised that there was a big change and the change was in me. I'd lost interest in my job. I didn't enjoy it as much and was already thinking about life beyond broking when we were told that we would have to cut head-count and one of the four staff on the desk would have to go.

I spoke to my long term colleague Richard privately as soon as we left the meeting and told him it would be me, secretly expecting it would be me anyway. There was a long winded procedure which I tried to circumvent my asking them if it *was* to be me, as I was happy to accept redundancy. However, because of my illness they had to go through the long winded and correct procedure and I understood that. I wasn't making much money, I was the oldest and the highest paid on the desk and indeed and I was indeed ill — although I don't like to admit it.

The company did the right thing and beyond. After several meetings with the directors and HR, it was decided that I was to go. They had a formula to assess all four of us and I came bottom. They asked me if I wanted to see the results, but I was happy to leave and we sat down to talk over terms. Their offer was indeed generous and took into account the fact that I had private medical cover. Tullett Prebon were very fair to me from beginning to end and I was happy to leave.

I left the final meeting about my redundancy and walked out of the building without going back to my desk. All of my things were couriered to my house later in the day. The motorcycle wasn't with me on that last day so I left the building by the front door and I looked back. I knew then, as I know now, that that was it for me. For thirty-two years I'd been a money broker. I'd had some of the best times anybody could have had in any job.

Through work, I'd lived in London, New York, Sydney and Singapore. I travelled first class around the world, stayed in the best hotels, ate in the best restaurants, drank some of the most ludicrously expensive wines and earned decent money. I had a great money broking career, and you won't ever hear me knocking that industry.

It is a strange job for many reasons but for me the most important thing about it were the people; it was always about the people. Two of my best friends are former customers from the early days. I have a few others that I would also call friends that I've met in later years. Some of the people I've dealt with I have really liked and some I've not liked, but they were all part of the rich tapestry. After all, they paid me well, which enabled me to enjoy a fantastic lifestyle over many years.

A few of my customers called me the day I left to make sure I was happy about the whole thing and to make sure Tullett Prebon had looked after me. I reassured them that I was fine and that Tullett Prebon had bent over backwards to make sure I was all right.

Then there were the calls from my ex-competitors. It was difficult to know where they were coming from exactly. Did they just want to know something or did they genuinely want to offer me a job? Did they think I was going to spill the beans? I didn't know; frankly, I didn't care. I was out and I wasn't going back. After a very short time I would be history.

I was actually offered two jobs, one in the UK and one abroad. The conversations were brief as I had no interest in the opportunities, but it was good to know that people still thought I had something to offer. *Did* I still have something to offer the financial markets? I didn't think so. As far as I was concerned those days were gone.

I'd been at Tullett Prebon for almost five years after leaving my previous employer, ICAP. With hindsight, I should have left the market when I left ICAP. Truthfully, I didn't have a great final five years as a broker. I earned less than I had done for a while and I didn't enjoy it as much as I'd used to. But you do what you think is right at the time and I had a mortgage to pay and a family to look after.

It was with an unexpected feeling of ease and contentment that I finally walked away from the building. My emotions were mixed because I knew that I would have to make money, I had a mortgage to pay and other bills. I certainly wasn't in any way rich, but I felt a true sense of calm and relief to be honest.

I also thought a lot about my health and what I'd been through in the last few months. I did worry though, as I knew that the same people who had been so upset after the diagnosis were now going to be worried about me being jobless.

Hazel and I sat down and had a long chat. She was more worried about the predicament than I was. At that point, I had an idea of what I was going to do but we hadn't really talked it over in depth. As you now know, there had been a few other things on our plates apart from the day jobs.

We worked out our financial position and how long we could survive on the redundancy money I was given. I'd already decided what I wanted to do. I was fifty-four years old, qualified as a scuba and first aid instructor, but I'd only ever worked for someone else, always an employee. Now, I was going to have to be a businessman and start my own company. I was excited and scared.

All my official working life I'd worked for companies. Here I was, starting a new chapter in my life and not just a new career. I wasn't even sure about the options I had. Because of programmes like Dragons' Den and people like Richard Branson, entrepreneurship seemed to be the way to go. For some reason I just couldn't see me putting on a suit and going for interviews.

So, I was going to be a businessman. It still makes me smile now: Kim the businessman.

We decided that we would take some time and have a proper think about life going forward. I was pretty convinced that I could make some money as a first aid instructor if I started my own company, which I did; First Aid Development. As this was something I've never done before it was going to be a new adventure and there would be a lot of learning to do.

I'd said for a long time that if I ever left the market, now that Jack and Nathan were over eighteen and old enough to make their own way in life, Hazel and I would sell up here and go to live in Australia. I lived there for almost ten years and have citizenship. The only problem was, Pazopanib wasn't available in the equivalent of the NHS there and as such, I would have to fund it privately, which would be fine for a short time while I had money from the redundancy. But long term, it could be very expensive.

So, for the moment, we were destined to stay here in good old Blighty, set up the company and get on with it.

I was very excited at the prospect on the one hand and completely daunted on the other. If there were such a thing as a third hand, I'd say I was also scared as scared could be!

It was great having all these ideas, and there were plenty of them, but I still had my health to look after. As I've continued this story you may have noticed that I refer less and less to my health. The reason is, I was getting better and better. The side effects were more controlled, the amount of drugs were reduced and generally I was feeling stronger and stronger. I certainly didn't let the cancer influence either what I was going to do or how I was going to do it.

My last official day in the market was the last day of April 2014. It was very strange as I walked out of the office and I knew in my heart that that was it.

May 2014 was spent working out how to be a company. There's a lot to consider as I'd lived in a bubble world for thirty-two years. If I'd needed anything as a broker, I asked and it was provided. Now I was going to have to be a bit of everything.

A friend, Nick Smith, suggested I attended a business-to-business event called Guildford Means Business. I went and was asked on the door for my company name. We had kicked a few names around, but First

Aid Development was sort of established finally at that moment.

I was a bit of a lost soul that day. All these different businesses, involved in so many different industries. I struggled to think that I too would be competing out there in the 'real' world. The real world did frighten me. Where and how do I get customers? Where and how do I set up? Where and how do I do almost everything!

One thing was for sure: cancer and I were going to start a company. I was excited at the prospect, but wasn't sure where to start. So, Hazel, Bryan and I had a top level meeting to put together a business plan. We did this whilst scuba diving in Egypt, which isn't the obvious thing to do when you're jobless, but it did give me a week clear of everything to think things over.

Chapter Nineteen

Taking cancer on holiday with me, again

As I've mentioned, I'm a PADI Master Suba Diver Trainer. As a diving professional, you have to have a strict dive medical every year. Without it, you can't teach anything in the water.

I explained to my dive doctor, Mark Downs, exactly what had happened and he said we would go through the normal procedures with no allowance for the cancers. You have to go to a specific dive doctor and not to your regular GP for a dive medical. These doctors are well versed in the additional considerations when scuba diving and are cleared to issue HSE approved medicals. I'm very glad to say, I passed with flying colours, which prompted a cry and a dance around the kitchen with Hazel on my return home from the medical!

Before going to Egypt, I had a meeting with the Prof and again, he suggested that I come off the Pazopanib for the week whilst I was away. So, as with skiing, I took a break from the Pazopanib, but continued with the blood pressure pills and anything else that I needed should any side effects continue. The side effects did abate quite quickly and we had the best week away you could imagine.

Bryan is a very competent rescue diver and Hazel is an experienced advanced diver. As such I was diving with people I know and trust so I could really relax and enjoy the dives.

There were a few things I had to be careful of. Scuba diving can dehydrate you and the weather in Egypt is very hot. So, note to self, plenty of water and little booze. The other thing I had to be careful of was the sun. My skin was and still is very sensitive and I was very aware that I could burn under the clear Egyptian skies.

We went to a resort called Marsa Nakari, on the shores of the Red Sea, and stayed in 'Royal' tents just metres from the sea.

When we arrived the place was deserted, apart from the twenty-one staff. The truth was, we were the only paying customers, and as such, we had the place to ourselves for the first few days. We had a minimum of two dives a day planned for six days. I'd already decided that I would dive as little or as much as I felt I could. This was my first serious dive trip since the operation, even though I'd done a few local dives back in the UK.

I cannot tell you how excited I was when we first put our gear on and jumped into the 'rib' (ridged hulled inflatable boat) for our first dive. Any thoughts of cancer, illness, drugs and side effects were gone. I was almost overcome with emotion.

Our first dive was to be an easy fifty minutes or so, depending on air consumption and conditions. The rib would take us out and we would make our way back to shore to do a beach exit. As experienced divers, we could probably stay longer and we had a flexible dive plan with the shore exit. Maybe a bit longer, maybe shorter. I was fit enough to dive, a medical had proved that, but I still wasn't really sure how I would get on.

We surfaced after just under an hour and that was only because we had reached the shore. We were well within the safe limit of available air and I could have stayed longer. Divers who read this will understand: when the underwater realm puts on a show, nothing can beat it.

For the non-divers reading this, two things. Firstly, you will only get to see about twenty-five per cent of this beautiful planet from dry land and television or cinema is no substitute for getting wet. Secondly, get yourself certified and go diving. It really should be on everyone's bucket list. Words and photos really don't do the underwater world justice.

Diving in Egypt with Hazel and Bryan.

We finished the dive and it was very emotional. Luckily, my face was already wet as the tears flowed. Happy tears, tears of relief, excitement, achievement and a realisation that the world was still there for me to enjoy. It was another goal I'd set and managed to achieve. I was doing it regardless of everything that had happened to date and cancer had to come with me, on my terms. I could not wait to get back into the water. And so we did, a further seventeen times that week.

This dive trip also included something very special: being in the water with dolphins.

We'd been to and dived Dolphin House Reef once before on a previous trip to Egypt, when we could hear the dolphins clicking but didn't see them. I've done thousands of dives over the years all around the world, but had never been in the water with dolphins.

We motored out to Dolphin House Reef on a dive boat in a party of about eighteen. As we moored at the dive site there was a large pod of (sleeping) dolphins. Amazingly, these fantastic creatures can close one eye, and one side of their brain shuts down to sleep for twenty minutes or so. Then they wake the sleeping side up and do the same with the other side. As mammals, they have to breathe air so they can't go to sleep like us, otherwise they would drown.

We could only snorkel with them from the ribs. Unfortunately, this would leave me very exposed to the sun (even with sun factor on) and I considered staying on the dive boat in the shade. However, as those wonders of the sea swam around us I couldn't resist it. I got on the rib, with snorkel gear and underwater camera in hand, and forgot everything else.

We entered the water and snorkelled with them. There were maybe twenty or thirty dolphins, maybe more, young and old. You can't keep up with them, so you just have to hope that they will swim to you if they want — and they did. Since I was first diagnosed, I cannot remember a time when cancer was further from my mind. In fact, if you ask me to remember a happy place, then this was it.

I don't know exactly how long we were with them; they eventually moved out from the reef to hunt. At which point we returned to the boat ecstatic! After pulling ourselves together we donned our scuba diving gear and went for couple of dives. The entire site is fantastic: brightly coloured corals, varied and various fish life everywhere and caves, anything and pretty much everything you would want. Plus, I'd been swimming with dolphins now as well. I've always had a special place in my heart for dolphins, it seems to be the same for a lot of people. I don't know what it is, maybe the ever smiley facial expressions or their intelligence — truly amazing creatures.

All the other dives were fantastic, including some night dives. We were joined by other guests at the resort after the first few days of having the reef to ourselves, which was fine. The ocean isn't ours really, although it felt as if we had borrowed it for a couple of days.

When we arrived home I returned to the normal drug regime, although this time I did notice a couple of differences. When we'd been skiing and I then returned to the drugs, I really hadn't noticed too many changes — but this time it was different. Maybe the longer break had made a difference.

Over a year, the metallic taste I had all the time abated a bit, but it returned when I started back on the Pazopanib after the dive trip. My blood pressure was a little higher, although this settled down after a couple of days. I'd kept out of the sun as much as possible, but my skin was more sensitive again and pressure on my hands when trying to grip things was increased. Also, the diarrhoea came back with a vengeance.

In total I'd been off the Pazopanib for ten days, the longest period since I had started taking it. Re-taking it triggered the same side effects I had suffered in the early days, but to a much lesser extent. This was the last time I was to take a break from the drugs, because I was learning how to adjust and cope with side effects better and the 'new normal' was indeed, quite normal.

Chapter Twenty

A new adventure

All of my official working life I've worked for somebody else. Margnor Fasteners, Motorist Discount Centre and thirty-two years as a money broker which in the end boiled down to two companies, Tullett Prebon and ICAP.

When it came to starting/owning/running a company I was utterly clueless. I didn't want to go back into the market and I really wasn't qualified to do much else so I took the skills I'd gathered over the last few years and First Aid Development was born.

I spent time researching whether there was any money to be made from first aid, what I would need to do to get set up, and who my customers were likely to be.

I'm an independent instructor trainer with a certification from Emergency First Response (EFR), who are owned by PADI, the Professional Association of Diving Instructors. I'm also a Master Scuba Diver Trainer with PADI, a manual handling instructor. Linking the first aid, I'm also able to instruct on Emergency Oxygen use. (An MSDT scuba instructor can teach specialist courses like deep dive, wreck diving or nitrox use.)

Funnily enough, I didn't want to teach scuba in this country. As I've grown older I seem to prefer easier diving and I'm not a fan of some inland dive sites. What I did want to teach was the first aid. A lot of my friends and family are self-employed or run their own companies so I did a lot of listening and, slowly, Hazel and I hatched a plan.

We knew we couldn't compete with the national first aid providers so we would have to specialise. EFR are one of the biggest first aid agencies in the world with over 56,000 instructors, but they don't have the same sort of set-up as the well-known agencies in the UK. I am an independent instructor trainer.

So we decided to find our own little niche. We could travel to customers, we could teach all the courses and we could be competitive. We also have experience, because I first qualified as a first aider in 1989 and as an advanced first aider the same year. I qualified as a first aid instructor in 2009 and as an instructor trainer in 2011.

As I said earlier, I attended a business forum called Guildford Means Business. I really did feel out of my depth, among all those companies and all sorts of services. This was a whole new world to me and I had so much learning to do.

This is how the world works: small businesses provide services to similar-sized or bigger companies. Tradesmen and women, service providers, lawyers... boy, did I have a lot to learn!

A friend, Stephen Surrey, suggested that I join BNI (Business Network International) as it would help to give the fledgling company some profile and I would be able to learn from the businesses there. He really was keen, almost to the point of pushy, about me joining, because BNI had saved his own garage from extinction in 2010.

At that point I had some old fashioned ideas about a small company, fully expecting to have to do a lot of door-to-door marketing to companies and the public. I'm glad Stephen prodded me into BNI because it has without a doubt leap-frogged my growth and business knowledge.

The format is a breakfast meeting which starts at 7am, although most people arrive at 6.30am. Full English breakfast, tea, coffee and juice. Lots of talking and discussing business and businesses.

Every week you get a chance to pitch or talk about your business for sixty seconds and, on a rotation basis, you get a chance to further expand people's knowledge by giving a ten-minute presentation. There's also an education slot which helps fellow members with their networking and general business skills.

I went along a couple of times and was very buoyed up by the response I received, both personally and as a new businessman. I joined BNI in August 2014 and, apart from three weeks to date, I've been there for every meeting. And of those three, only one was due to illness.

After I'd been going for a couple of months I did my own ten-minute presentation. For the first time the whole group got to know that I have cancer, although a few people had known beforehand. I was very proud of my presentation which included a personal history, my business and how I was going to move it forward.

What I was most pleased with was a couple of PowerPoint slides... I had asked permission to use the Macmillan font and colour, and the charity had agreed only to my use of their colour — so in that very evocative shade of green, my slide said: "Living with Cancer."

As I put the slide up and explained the cancer malarkey to the forty-odd people in the group, their faces fell. However, the next slide was: "Cancer — Trying to live with Kim!" in large, bright green letters. This has very much become my mantra and I use it a lot. That broke the tension

Over the next couple of slides there were photos of Hazel and me skiing, scuba diving, on the motorcycle and camping, all with the precursor of: "We have dragged cancer..." followed by the photo.

I'm also a member of another networking group called Best of Guildford which runs in a similar way to BNI.

By August 2014 I was really well. There were side effects but they were increasingly well controlled and I needed to take fewer drugs for them. I hardly saw the GP at all.

These days, when I meet people and the topic comes up, I tell them I have cancer and they find it difficult to believe because I do not look like an ill person. Outwardly, the only thing the keen eye would notice is the white goatee beard, eyelashes and, to a lesser extent these days, eyebrows. People who've never met me before I became what I am, can *never* tell. Cancer is a git. It hides and grows and you only find out when it becomes difficult to combat.

One thing I've said to many people is: "If I could hard-wire you into my head, you would see I'm fine. I'm in a good place." The thing is, I'm in pretty good shape physically and in a very good place mentally.

People ask me all the time how I'm feeling and the majority of times I reply by saying I'm fine. I know they don't believe me or think that I can't be *that* well. The truth is, for the most part, I am.

I launched myself into the business world, learning as I went along. It seems that everybody's business is different, just like everybody's cancer.

I've met a lot of people up to this point in my new life, and in meeting people and talking with them, several of them suggested I write this book. I must say I've always wanted to write a book but it wasn't going to be *this* one. So maybe there's more to come.

Writing it has not been easy though. It's the emotions that are difficult, and re-reading my diary and remembering, especially the early days of the diagnosis, have been very upsetting. I've had to stop many times whilst writing this — sometimes just to clear my head for five minutes, sometime for hours or days. I didn't want the book to drag me down. Even though the cancer hasn't, re-living the whole event over and over again can take its toll. It's like picking at a very tender scab.

The first year was a big learning curve and a personal journey, as I've said. I was moving into my second year now on the Pazopanib. By now though, I'd been through most of the side effects and even though some were tamed, I also knew others would be with me as long as I stayed on the drug.

I didn't really know whether the second year would be any different to the first and in fact, there is no time frame — it's just life. The one thing that will never change is the fact that the cancer is always there and sometimes gives me a little nudge to remind me. I will get nausea, or one of the other side effects will rear its head.

The best thing is that I have experience with my cancer and my daily and monthly regime is a well-trodden path now.

Chapter Twenty-one

Moving on

There are many things I've learned in the last couple of years. You think you're ahead of the game, but every so often cancer gives you a nudge just to let you know it's still around.

For me, this is every three to four months when I have to go for the CT scans. As I've said before, the scan itself is pretty simple and painless, but emotionally it can get on top of you. There's no escape and every time the CT scan comes around it brings it home to me with a wallop.

The other sort of milestone for me was the daily journal I'd been keeping. Up to this point I've quoted various days from it and used it as a marker for events. I wrote everything down religiously for the first year. Every day, everything. Blood pressure, temperature, heart rate, oxygen saturation and a short diary of events, good and bad.

After a year I moved it back to a weekly summary, usually at the weekends. The reason was that the side effects were pretty constant and I'm pleased to say that by November 2014, into my second year with cancer, I had stopped writing a journal completely.

Every month I still have to go to St Luke's Cancer Centre for blood tests. The following day I have an appointment with Professor Pandha. We go through the blood tests, I get weighed and my blood pressure is recorded.

I can only get the Pazopanib from the oncology unit at St Luke's. These drugs are very expensive and powerful. If my blood tests showed that I wasn't coping with the drugs then they would be stopped — either for a while, or in order to try a different drug.

For the most part my blood results are excellent and, as such, I get another month of drugs. There are a few quirks in my tests but through the Prof's experience and close monitoring, we are aware of the true picture of my health. The best news for me is that my remaining kidney and adrenal gland seem to be doing fine.

I would like at this point to say that even though I mostly see Professor Pandha, he has a number of registrars whom I also see and there's always an oncological nurse on hand as well. The service from both the private and NHS sectors are truly remarkable. I know there are a few nay-sayers but from personal experience, the medical teams have been fantastic.

Of course, I still get a lot of advice from people about alternative medicines. It is invariably well-intended but in my world they don't work and here's why:

For the most part the alternative medicines are badly researched if they are researched at all. A lot of the evidence is anecdotal and not backed up by clinical trials. There's also no admission that the people trying the alternatives have already had any other treatments, either chemical or natural. It's too ad hoc and unreliable for me.

A clinical drug such as the type I'm on takes between ten and twenty years to get on to the market, with many trials, and tens of millions of pounds invested, before being approved. I have confidence in my drug for that very reason and the improved survival rates for metastatic kidney cancer speak for themselves. More than eighty per cent is great odds! A lot of alternative drugs are for the best part un-tested — or I should say, not thoroughly enough tested under proper clinical conditions.

The same people who promote alternative treatments often have a big problem with the pharmaceutical companies and the profits they make. They argue that cancer treatment is all about the money.

Is this really the case though? Well, the drug companies *are* businesses and indeed, they need to make money. But the first step is the drug company finding a potential cure or treatment, which they immediately patent, and then they research it. They have to sink millions and millions into the research and finally, *if* successful, they are granted a licence to market the drug.

Here's a thing to add to the drug company's risk: only one in twenty drugs makes it to the market. Add to this the fact that in the first instance, the drug company took out a patent, if it's taken fifteen years or more to get the drug to market, they only have five years to make money from it as most patents only last for twenty years. These facts are well documented, but many people wish to ignore them as it makes their argument against the pharmaceutical companies stronger.

I have a number of problems with the alternative regime. If I were to give up my proven drug, that's obviously working well, and started with alternative drugs, they *might* help me — but if they don't, I can't buy back that wasted time.

The 'information' used to vilify the medical establishment can be amusing, seriously sad and, at times, blatantly misleading. Quoting reports from the 1930s and the research that was done then into cancer is of course ridiculous. We have moved on and we now know more about cancer than we've ever known. We have the human genome and know the DNA of cancer. Research has come on in leaps and bounds over the last few years.

I often get the same thing expressed to me about the pharmaceutical companies. I'm told they suppress all the alternative medicines so they can make big profits. Well, if it really was that easy to cure cancer then the governments could collect the magic ingredient from the forest, put a label on it, market it and sell it. Do people honestly think that there are genuine cures out there that are not being used? After all, the burden to the health systems worldwide are vast and governments all need to save money. I'm sure you've read the conspiracy theories.

A lot of people who push alternative medicine still run to the NHS when they are diagnosed. I do wonder why, if they believe they already have the cures. However, I do think in some cases that an alternative or additional regime can be helpful. After all there are patients on traditional chemotherapy and other treatments who need help to revitalise their immune systems.

There are a few things that are being looked at as having potential as cures for cancer. Cannabis oils for instance are now being clinically tested, and as far as I know the early results are encouraging. So I don't close my mind to everything. I do listen because there are things out there that are of value, just don't try to sell them to me until there is some documented clinical proof that they work.

The one thing that really worries me are the unscrupulous people who sell their 'cures' to all sorts of vulnerable people, not just to cancer patients.

There is one sort of alternative regime that I do adopt wholeheartedly, which is a mental attitude to my illness. And if a positive mental attitude *is* an alternative regime, then I hold my hands up — I totally agree with the power of the mind.

Which brings me to another phase of my life — Immunotherapy.

Chapter Twenty-two

Immunotherapy

Professor Pandha is head of clinical oncological research at the University of Surrey and has a team of scientists working with him. He's been very patient with all my questions about Pazopanib and the newer drugs on the market.

Immunotherapy is his research area, not only into kidney cancer but *all* cancers because the basis of his research is the use of our own immune system to fight and kill cancer.

Here's the thing: cancer is clever and moreover it's part of you. As such, your immune system doesn't recognise it as being a problem and passes it by. It is a very complicated science. What they've been researching is a way to boost your immune system so it can recognise the cancer and destroy it.

If they can find answer to this, then the more traditional treatments of radio and chemo therapies, which can cause shocking collateral damage, need be used less and less. If we can use our own immune system, then we really are getting closer to surviving cancer. The big bonus is the fact that if we use our immune system, there are very few side effects.

The good news, the brilliant news, is *they have*! And from a source you really wouldn't have suspected. Viruses.

The subject is very complicated and I do not have enough knowledge to explain it fully. But, in the most general of terms, what's been discovered is that cancers can't cope with a virus.

Some of the world's nastiest viruses are now being genetically modified and injected into a cancer tumour. The virus replicates quickly and explodes out of the cell, exposing the cancer to our immune system, which very efficiently attacks, kills and clears out the cancer. Once our immune system recognises a problem then it has a memory for it. Just as we never get exactly the same cold twice, our immune system remembers the problem and automatically fights it anywhere in the body.

This research isn't new but at last it's getting proper recognition and funding. There are many different avenues being investigated, and in some cases there are ongoing clinical trials. One question that's being asked is, how long will your immune system 'remember' the cancer? We don't know yet, but we do now have an additional weapon in our armoury thanks to the research being conducted and mostly paid for by the pharmaceutical companies.

In addition, an even newer approach is being developed to fight cancer. As I've said, cancer is clever and hides from your immune system; it has a sort of invisibility cloak. The latest development, called a check point inhibitor (PD-1, PD-L1), breaks down the cancer cells' ability to hide and allows them to be exposed to your immune system. Once exposed, your immune system is powerful enough to kill the cancer. This is a double-pronged attack, along with the virus therapy approach. We won't know for a long time why a cell mutates and becomes cancerous but for future generations, cancer won't be the demon it's been for so long to so many people. The landscape is changing.

One of the many questions I have asked Professor Pandha was about any charities I could support. The work he is involved in and his team are supported by a local charity — I want to tell you more about that.

Chapter Twenty-three

Topic of Cancer

From the early days of my treatments with Professor Pandha and his team, I've had an endless amount of questions for them. I'm very interested in cancer and medicine in general. In conversation with the Prof I asked if there was a charity he was involved in or that supported his work. I was keen to try and give something back in any way I could.

I've always given to charity, sadly less these days as I'm not earning money-market salaries, but Hazel and I still donate on a regular basis and to ad hoc events as well.

The Prof put me in touch with Nigel Lewis-Baker who is chair of Topic of Cancer (www.topicofcancer.org.uk), which he set up in Guildford just over two years ago, to support the work of Professor Pandha and his team at the university. They raise money for his research and to spread the word about the amazing work the research labs do. They also have support groups all over the country.

Even though Topic of Cancer is only two years old, it's managed to supply a couple of important pieces of equipment for the labs. But it's not all about expensive kit. Even simple things like Petri dishes cost money, and without even the most basic of items research cannot continue. The cost of disposables is large and all the items can only be used once. Some only cost pence, such as protective gloves, but without them there wouldn't be any research. This is very much the message I try to get out. I want people to know where their money goes.

As a small charity, everybody volunteers and, as such, almost all monies collected go straight to the research unit.

Nigel Lewis-Baker is a remarkable man. He was himself diagnosed with terminal inoperable prostate cancer almost eleven years ago. He's is still in good health after many and various trials. He received an MBE in December 2014 for his service to charity. Around him he has a tight-knit team of trustees and regional ambassadors. I'm proud to say that I'm now a trustee too, happily giving up time to help others.

The charity sector is a very different world and I'm very new to it. I have a lot to learn and the good news is the team we have are excellent. What I like about Topic of Cancer is that in supporting the research labs it's not organ-specific but focused on the new attacks on cancer. The research team are right at the front of UK research and are one of only three in the country.

There are thirteen viruses in clinical trials and the first is about to be released for advanced melanomas (skin cancer). The research team have also been at the forefront of research into a new prostate cancer test called EN2. This will revolutionise testing for prostate cancer, being a urine dip test that can be done at your local GP surgery — and it is significantly more accurate than the existing PSA blood test. The EN2 test is just awaiting a final stamp of approval from the FDA (Federal Drug Administration).

If you are interested in learning more, please look at our website www.topicofcancer.org.uk.

The charity not only supports the research labs, they also have local support groups around the country that meet every month. It is really good to be able to sit down with like-minded people to talk over worries, ideas and concerns. An example of this is body image.

Many patients undergo either major surgery or clinical trials and have body image problems. They don't want to go to a public gym or swimming pool. This is the sort of issue we want to address.

After I gave a talk at one of the support group meetings, one of the guests asked me for a private chat. He seemed too shy to ask me a question openly, even though he obviously had one. When we moved away from the crowded room a little, he asked me what it was like to be diagnosed with a terminal illness. I thought for a very brief second and then replied: "Like yours?"

He was taken aback and straight away denied any illness, especially anything terminal. I went on to explain that we are all dying, from the moment we're born in fact. The only difference between us was the fact I'd been diagnosed with a disease and given a label, he had not. He got my point. He nodded, smiled and shook my hand with vigour.

This made me think about my life prior to and post diagnosis. I've always had a fatalistic view of the world and most importantly, enjoying my life. My attitude since the diagnosis hasn't changed much: I still enjoy life and I want to be around a long time to enjoy even more.

A few people very close to me have cancer and I know that in many cases, the people who suffer the most emotionally are the carers. Obviously, this doesn't only apply to cancer patients and their carers; it applies to individuals suffering from many other diseases and the people who care for them. The patient gets lots of attention, tests, information and help. The carers are the silent backbone.

Neil Barber said to me at our very first meeting that I had a team around me. There was him and his team, the hospital staff and, when he'd finished and referred me on, it was the new team of Professor Pandha, his team and the staff at St Luke's. But the real team for me, and I can never thank her enough, is Hazel. I must also thank my family and my ever faithful friends for being part of my team.
Even if I live to be a hundred and earn millions of pounds, I won't ever be able to thank them all enough for their support. I feel very blessed.

Chapter Twenty-four

Who cares for the carers?

This chapter is a wider view of carers and not just about cancer.

I get a lot of attention. I have regular tests and many people know about my cancer journey which is of course unique to me. As you have seen so far, there are a lot of people who have come along on this bizarre ride. I have 'teams' that I can turn to for advice and help — and then there's the internet.

More than two and a half million people are living with cancer. Everyone with cancer needs someone to care for them and to support them: family, friends, doctors, nurses or the brilliant people at Macmillan Cancer Support, for instance. If you expand that to other diseases the number of carers is considerably larger. There are many diseases and conditions where, without the carers, life would be miserable.

I'm very lucky with my team and the brilliant support network around me. As I've said, they give me so much strength, all of them.

But I want to draw your attention for a moment to the Hazels of this world. For every sick person there are carers, sometimes multiple carers. They need support too! They need a shoulder to cry on and a net to fall into. Their lives are dogged with uncertainty and, in many cases, unpleasantness. They don't get asked how they are and they are often the forgotten angels.

I'm blessed in that that most people who ask me how I am, also ask about Hazel. It does worry me though that she (and others) go through the mill. I try to make sure she is OK and that her needs are met too. I involve her in everything, and for me there has always been one very important thing: the truth.

Sometimes it's difficult to *tell* the truth, but I can't hide from my cancer and I certainly won't run away from it, so I've always felt that the truth is really important. To this end, I have always been very honest about my illness, with myself and my loved ones.

From the carers' point of view, and I've been one myself, there is a lot of frustration. They want to make it right, they want to help more, and they often wish it was them, especially when the ill person is a child. I helped to look after my niece when she was diagnosed with Type 1 diabetes at the age of four and a half. Whenever you deal with children there's always an emotional loading as we are so programmed to look after and protect the young ones.

The carers also fend off questions, make appointments, meet and advise others in similar situations. They become a personal assistant in many ways.

Through my involvement with Topic of Cancer I've visited some very large charities that help not just the ill, but also the families. The range of services these charities offer, both large and small, is very humbling and amazing.

I was at a centre recently where they look after disabled children locally. They told me that once a week, a mum brings along a severely handicapped child for two hours. For those two hours, the mum sits in her car in the car park listening to music. It's the only respite she gets from being a round-the-clock mum, carer and lifeline to her son.

Where have I gone for advice over the last while?

My first port of call has always been the specialists: Neil Barber and his team and Hardev Pandha and his team. There are also my local GPs, the pharmacist, chiropodists and other clinicians I've seen for various maladies along the way.

I have never been refused information, I've never not been answered when I've asked about something, no matter how minor the worries. I have copies of all of my reports, blood tests and CT scans. As a layman, I am as up to date and informed as I can be. The information is there, all you have to do is ask for it — and I would encourage you to do so.

The internet is useful for research but I'm also very wary of it. I only use credible sites, mostly UK based, and even then some of the articles that are published turn out to be scams despite looking exactly like a genuine site.

I use The National Health Service website, Cancer Research UK and Macmillan Cancer Support websites. A lot of the charities have very useful websites with information and help. Many have support groups as well. There are also centres, some of which are a godsend. I only know of the ones local to me — the Foundation Centre and Phyllis Tuckwell Hospice — but you can find them all over the country.

I could probably fill another book with numbers and advice pages but all I would say is, please don't suffer in silence either as a patient or a carer. You are not alone!

Chapter Twenty-five

Cancer, the taboo word

Two years in and you would not believe the number of people who still won't talk to me about cancer. Sometimes they whisper it or say it under their breath. The other popular dodge is to refer to it just as 'C'. It's cancer, it's a disease, and there are many other diseases that kill people.

Cancer really is a taboo word and if we can break these taboos down then I am convinced more people will survive it.

If we were less worried, especially now when we have so many alternatives to the old fashioned methods of dealing with cancer, then people would go to their doctors and get diagnosed earlier. This would increase their chances of survival massively. You never want to hear something bad, but something bad now is better than something terminal later. Go and get yourself checked out.

My Dad was a classic example of this and I know far too many people who are just as scared and have left it too late.

Cancer is a big word, but I think hope is a bigger word — I *like* hope!

If you know what's wrong with you, then there's a chance to fix it. If you let it go by then it will only get worse.

So, what do you say to people with cancer or other complaints? Whatever you feel you should. Talk to them, ask them questions and above all be open. In many cases they want to talk and need to talk. Be a good listener — it really is very helpful, especially if you can tell them about your own emotions.

I am happy to talk about my cancer to anybody, whenever or whatever they want to know. I don't hide from it or hide anything about it from other people. I take strength from people who want to know — after all, they may be asking for themselves or a loved one and don't want to admit it.

My life has changed immeasurably over the last two years, arguably for the better.
I've learned a lot about myself, about the people around me and life in general. If I can, I want to help others now. Especially as I'm the healthiest ill person in the world.

As for cancer? It has to come along for the ride. I pay it little attention really, although I can't escape it totally. After two years, I still have an eleven-inch scar and my hair is predominately polar white (apart from my eyebrows — they have colour again). From time to time I have to take drugs to help with side effects when they come back.

I've been asked if I was scared of the cancer. No! I'm not scared of cancer, it doesn't frighten me and I'm not scared of death. The thing that does frighten me is not being able to live my life on my terms. Also the thought that my brilliant life will come to an end sooner rather than later gets to me as well.

Yet again, it's the emotions of the cancer and what's happened and happening that I've found difficult at times to come to terms with. It still really upsets me when I think of how it's affected people around me and what they've been through.

Chapter Twenty-six

A meeting with sharks and cancer

At the beginning of the book I said there was a connection between these two events. They are connected in my life and this is why.

On 28th May 1989 I was with my cousin David and our colleague Hoppy, out sailing in Sydney Harbour. Hoppy and I were going to do a couple of scuba dives off the boat. David isn't a scuba diver so he was going to stay on board and look after the boat. We had all the provisions you need for a dive and a sail: boat, scuba gear, beer (lots of), food (small amounts), check, check, check, check!

We sailed from Mosman harbour to North Head. The dive plan was to do a forty-minute dive at 'Old Man's Hat', which has plenty of colourful soft coral in the shallows and an enormous amount of sea life as you go deeper. The plan included a maximum depth limit of twenty-five metres, and lost buddy procedure and alternative exit just in case the yacht should break its anchor.

Tanks full, buddy checks done and Hoppy and I descended the anchor line with David watching us go. The day was clear, the swell a bit choppy, but it was

OK. In fact, it was a good day to dive. This dive was only my twelfth after qualifying as an open water scuba diver.

When we arrived on the sea bed, twenty-three metres down, the anchor was sitting on a huge flat rock. Hoppy signalled to move the anchor and chain into the sand to secure it. He grabbed the anchor and I grabbed the chain. What I didn't see was the five foot long Ornate Wobbygong shark lazing beside the anchor chain.

He was none too pleased with being wacked by a heavy chain and bit me. All of a sudden, I was being pushed backwards through the water with this shark attached to my right thigh, just above the knee! Beyond the shark, I could see Hoppy swimming the other way. I don't blame him, there was nothing much he could do without endangering himself.

Wobbygong sharks are bottom-feeding sharks that grow to about twelve feet in length. They eat lobster and crab by crushing them. They are generally harmless to divers, although clearly when disturbed, they behave like grumpy old men!

Fine, it's not a Great White and it doesn't have razor-sharp cutting teeth. It does, however, have a set of 'pencil' type gnashes which it uses to hold onto prey before it crushes them.

So there I was, with a shark attached to my leg... what page of the Open Water Manual was that on, then?

I wasn't going to go for my knife, as it was strapped to my other leg, just past the bitey end of the shark. My only thought was to hit it, so I punched it on the nose! Punched? Well, sort of hit it in slow motion. Whatever it was, it did the job and the shark let go, dumped me on the sea bed and swam off.

Thankfully, the shark hadn't made off with my leg; I could see it. There was no blood, although, annoyingly, there was damage to my new 5mm wetsuit. The one thing I had to attend to was, I was hyperventilating badly.

So far so good: I was in one piece. But, there was still twenty-three metres (seventy-five feet) of water above me and that could kill me in a much more efficient manner than the shark.

I sat and tried to control my breathing, watching my air content gauge. Hoppy returned and checked to see how bad I was — he'd seen the whole thing unfold. After a couple of minutes we made the world's slowest ascent to the surface, taking at least twice the time we would have normally taken. On surfacing beside the boat, my cousin leaned over and asked why we were back so quickly. "Kim's been bitten by a shark!" Hoppy announced.

David leaned into the water and pulled me and all my gear onto the boat in one go. I do wonder what went through his mind at that moment, as he couldn't have known how much of me he was going to pull out of the water!

My leg was now in a lot of pain, but that meant the feeling was back. Immediately after the attack, I'd had a 'dead leg' — very strange. I got my scuba gear off first, then took my new wetsuit off to reveal a massive bruise and six puncture wounds in my leg.

I was fine after all, I was alive. I had my leg, there were some holes in it and a bruise all over it. I hadn't had a 'dead leg' since I was at school, and when it first happened it did worry me.

The three of us had a high level meeting about the whole episode: I wanted to go for a sail, and they wanted me to go to hospital. My argument was that, after all, we had a lot of cold beer to drink, and I'd had a tetanus jab a little while ago. I won! We went for a sail and drank the beer.

Here's the exact dive log:

Date: 28/5/89
Dive Number: 12
Max. Depth: 23m
Location: North Head (Sydney)
Dive Buddy: Hoppy
Dive Type: Boat
Visibility: 3-4 metres
Tank Pressure in: 3400 psi. Tank Pressure out: 2500 psi
Dive Environment: Sandy and Rocky
Surface condition: Choppy

Comments or observations: Shark bite to right leg above the knee Ornate Wobbygong small cuts. No panic large use of air. Safe return to the surface. Dive aborted.
Bottom Time: 8 minutes

Why have I recounted this story?

On 15th May 2013, Hazel and I sat with Neil Barber in his office with a computer screen in front of us. On the screen was the CT scan of my torso showing the alien. Even to the untrained eye, it was obvious what we were seeing.

After the initial shock of being told, Neil started to explain the options. The best one by far, in his considered opinion, was to get rid of the alien.

He explained the procedure and said that, all things being equal, the tumour would be removed and he was expecting a ten-inch scar which would be glued. He said the scar would be large but neat, a bit like a shark bite...

I looked up and casually told him I'd already had one of those. He frowned, smiled and then asked: "Really?" Yes, I said, on my leg years ago while I was diving.

"You're not joking, are you?" he said. "No", I replied.

Hazel then said: "I bet you've never had *that* reaction before to that comment."

He was taken aback initially, as you would expect. After the light moment and some more explanations, we returned to the topic at hand: metastatic renal cancer.

That explains the title of this book: *A meeting with sharks and cancer*. You can, indeed, meet and survive both!

I've told this story many times now and I hope Mr Barber has too — even in the darkest of times there's humour to be rescued from it.

The following chapter is Hazel's. It struck me that there were always two views of this journey and mine is biased, because it's mine. I wanted her to write what she felt and what she's been through. I've not edited it in any way and although at times it might repeat some of the things I've already said — I think it's an important part of this book for you to read.

Chapter Twenty-seven

Hazel's view

I didn't worry too much at the beginning when he first found the 'lump' (alien). I don't do panic or drama. *Don't panic until there is something to panic about* has always been my mantra. Even when there is something to panic about, I can't bear drama, hysteria or fuss. That's more about attention seeking than trying to deal with a problem or situation you find yourself in.

So, it was not until Kim had the ultrasound scan indicating an undetermined 'lump' on his kidney that I started to be concerned, in a calm way. I went with him for the initial consultation with the urology department at the Royal Surrey Hospital, to the CT scan and then to the follow-up appointment with Mr Barber at Spire Clare Park Hospital, Farnham.

I honestly remember very little of the conversation in that office. When Mr Barber was reviewing the scan on screen he stopped when he got to the offending 'lump'. I think the world stopped turning at that point, mine did anyway. I will never forget that image — it was everything I feared most, staring out at me from a computer screen. Talk of cutting it out, large scars and shark bites followed. It all sounded very straightforward. I guess if you are doing this kind of thing day in day out, it *is* all very straight forward.

Then, the written report from the radiologist was delivered. Mr Barber read it out and the next blow hit us. There were more tumours, six in the lungs and two on lymph nodes. My world was collapsing in slow motion around me. There I was, sitting in a lovely office, in the very pleasant private hospital that is Clare Park, in its beautiful green surroundings, whilst my world was falling apart.

Kim and Mr Barber were talking of the technicalities of the operation and follow-up treatments, how he would remove the tumour, when he would remove the tumour. Kim loves all the medical stuff and it felt like they were talking about someone else, someone unknown, not involved, but this was about *my husband*, this was all about Kim.

I just sat and stared at that screen. I hadn't spoken, I don't think I was really listening, just staring at the image on the screen, I have no idea how long for. Then I was asked if I had any questions. I couldn't form words, nothing would come out. I just about managed: "No, not at the moment."

Obviously, it was not what I said, it was how I said it. The box of tissues was handed to me. I'm scared. Don't panic, it will all be OK. Keep telling yourself that and it will be all right.

We drove home, mostly in silence, which is most unlike us. So much was going around in my head, I was unable to verbalise it at that stage. It is like being hit, side-on, by a juggernaut. I felt winded, sick. Kim said: "It's a lot to take in, isn't it?" I would say it's more like a f**king massive amount to take in and I can't do it all in one go, it's just too big and I'm too small!

I hated that day, and it got worse, if that were even possible. We were both calling family and friends to tell them the news. So many tears, so much upset. I hated telling my parents, they worry so much. I knew they would be devastated; I am convinced they like Kim more than me! (Don't panic, it will all be OK.)

I wanted to hide, pretend it wasn't happening. That didn't work. I can remember telling people about Kim's cancer but, even then, not really believing it all myself. It didn't seem real. It took a while to truly sink in, to realise all the implications. (I'm scared. Don't panic, it will all be OK.)

The next day, with the blessing of Mr Barber, we did the most sensible thing we could think of when given such news. We jumped on a motorcycle and rode to France!

We had been before, we love the motorbike trips, we love the Moto GP, we love going away with our friends. All the right ingredients, but how could we possibly enjoy it? How could it be the same? More than that, how could we enjoy anything ever again? How could life ever be the same again? The fear was starting to creep in. Kim has cancer. I'd never been so scared in my life, it was all consuming. (Don't panic, it will all be OK.)

We had a good trip down through France with Bryan and Lorraine. We always have such great times with them. Still having fun, still laughing, but it wasn't the same. I couldn't shift that underlying feeling, the big knot that had formed inside me. I might be smiling on the outside, but not on the inside.

We arrived at the hotel to meet the others. We would be in the company of good friends. As we walked towards the door of the hotel, I knew they would be in the bar (if we are not at the track then we are in the bar, obviously!). I got to the door and another overwhelming notion hit me, one that I hadn't expected... please don't treat us differently. I felt different, but I so wanted to feel normal. Please don't treat us differently, don't feel sorry for us, no fuss. We walked in to be greeted by big smiles, big hugs and: "Do you want a vodka and tonic?" So, situation normal, such relief. Thank you, thank you, thank you good friends.

The month between the meeting with Mr Barber and the operation was horrendous. The anxiety of knowing what was coming, knowing what was inside him, but not knowing how it was all going to turn out and not knowing how Kim was going to be after the operation. During that month of waiting no one was helping him, no one was trying to make him better. It seemed like a very, very long month.

I handed in my notice in at work, which was more upsetting than I had anticipated. I'd been with the company for ten years and was very sad to be leaving. However, I felt that I could not possibly do my job and look after Kim. We had no idea what the recovery period would be like, how long and what kind of condition he would be in. We had visions of 24/7 nursing. So, it was best to leave the job. I could always get another job at some point in the future, depending on how Kim's recovery went. He was my priority.

My head was in a mess. For someone who doesn't do drama, it all felt very dramatic. What would I do if I lost him? Die. If he dies, so do I. I don't want a life without him. I will simply curl up and cease to be. But I can't do that, he would be so angry and disappointed with me. I have two children, albeit they are young adults, but I still have a responsibility to be here for them. So I'd sell the house, give Jack and Nathan enough to get them started in life and go. Go and do all the things we would do if we won the Lottery! Climb Kilimanjaro, kayak down the Amazon, jump out of an aeroplane at 15,000 feet, do a ski season, work in a dive centre in the Maldives. Whatever, just do it all until my body falls to bits and I can do it no more!

So much change and so much turmoil. It is life changing, but not in a winning-the-Lottery kind of way. It was all-consuming, suffocating, terrifying. I would go out with friends and feel detached, abnormal, again smiling on the outside but not on the inside. It wouldn't go away, there was no respite. It is in your head all of the time, it's all you can think about. I'm so scared... Don't panic, it will all be all right... I've got to be strong for him...

I wanted to be treated normally, I wanted to feel normal. I wanted to ignore it. Please treat me normally. Don't tell me I'm too thin, I can't help it. Should I drink, should I not? Will it make me feel better? Will it make me feel worse? Oh, please, please give me some release from my own mad head!

Finally, the day arrived to go to hospital. The room was lovely, the surgeon, anaesthetist, doctors, nurses were all so kind and reassuring. You felt in safe hands. I was scared though. (Don't panic, it will all be OK. Be strong for Kim.) I hated saying goodbye as he was taken to surgery. He was gone for hours and I sat in the room alone. It seemed like an eternity, reading, watching television, anything to occupy my mind. I was worried, but confident that all would go to plan.

When it was finished he was in recovery before going into the intensive care unit. I was allowed to go to see him in recovery. He was fine, completely conscious, but numb from the chest down. He was better than I had thought he would be. Great staff, great care. I stayed with him for about an hour, by which time he was ready for some sleep and they were moving him from recovery into ICU for the night, so time for me to leave. I didn't want to go.

Bryan and Lorraine invited me to stay with them for the duration of Kim's stay in hospital. Jack remained at home on his own; it was easier for him to get to work from home and, at twenty, he was perfectly capable of looking after himself (apparently)! Nathan was working with Bryan at the time, so it made sense for him to stay at theirs too. It was such a good idea. I could go back to theirs from the hospital each day without having to worry about things like cooking or cleaning. I would walk in the door each evening, have a shower, change into slouch pants and slippers, be handed a glass of wine and sit down to a meal. Bless them, they looked after me so very, very well, both physically and emotionally.

The next day, the big operation. I arrived at the hospital early and went into ICU to spend some time with Kim before going to surgery. Mr Barber came to see him and talk through the operation and confirmed that he was in the theatre that had a camera, so the operation could be filmed. I wonder how many people there are who want to watch themselves being operated on? One thing that I certainly never anticipated doing in my life was watching hours and hours of footage of my husband being operated on, from scalpel to sutures. How many wives can say: "I've seen my husband's liver"? I really do know him inside and out now.

It was extremely difficult to leave him that morning. I was holding it together well until he said: "If it all goes wrong, promise me you will carry on having fun without me." I was very scared and anxious, but confident that he was in extremely safe hands. Lorraine came to the hospital to meet me once Kim had been taken to theatre. We went to the coffee shop, chatted about anything and everything (we are quite good at that!), then went back up to Kim's room and watched television. Hours and hours and hours of waiting. I was terrified. (Don't panic, it will all be OK. Be strong.)

Mr Barber came to see us after he had finished and said that it had all gone very well. It was 'unremarkable', which is just what you want to hear. Lorraine left at that point, after all she had a life of her own to get on with. I had to wait a little longer and then went down to ICU to see Kim.

It was very different this time. He was wired up to all sorts of equipment and monitors. A bank of screens next to him, tubes all over the place. If you have never been into an ICU, it can be daunting. It was very upsetting to see the person I love most in life in that condition, but such a relief that he had come through the operation so well. Kim was good, much better than I had expected, but it felt like he was trying too hard. He was so determined to get through it and not have everyone worry about him. He was trying to prove to the world that he was just fine. I didn't know whether to be pleased and relieved or to worry. The constant monitoring was encouraging; we were reading off his blood pressure every ten minutes from the screen like it was a darts score! So, due to good 'behaviour', he was allowed to go back to his room for the night rather than stay in ICU for another night.

Over the five days that he was in the hospital I lived life like it was someone else's. It was surreal, nothing like my life had been up to now. Being in hospital is like living in a bubble, the real world is outside somewhere. You are surrounded by the experts, those that know what to do when there is a problem, as I witnessed on day three when I thought Kim was having a good sleep, but in reality he was slipping into a coma! One minute I was tiptoeing around the room trying not to wake him and the next he was surrounded by nurses and doctors, putting in lines, cold flannel on his head, a fan and oxygen mask. It all happened so quickly I didn't have a chance to panic.

When the day came to take him home, it was with some trepidation. Now I was going to be responsible for looking after the patient. There is no nurse's station at fifteen paces down the corridor at home. He was far better than we had anticipated, but I was still concerned. (I'm scared. Don't panic, it will all be OK. Be strong.)

So, we started life post-op, pre-Pazopanib. He was remarkable. He was ridiculous! He didn't know he was supposed to be ill. Actually, he has never known, realised or accepted that he is supposed to be ill. It just isn't there in his mind set, which has proved to be the most important part of *my* ability to cope. He has been so strong and that has made *me* strong. I can't show him up, I can't let the side down; if he can be this brilliant then so must I. I'm not going to be the pathetic one weeping in the corner. We are a team.

Taking the drugs hasn't always been easy for him. He has had some very difficult days, which means that I have had some very difficult days, because we are a team. But my husband is a very stubborn, strong and determined man. At times that can be difficult to live with. "This is not a marriage, it is a dictatorship," is a phrase I have used, happily only once in thirteen years. However, these are qualities that can be useful when you are trying to kick cancer in the arse!

I have had to dig deep and find inner strength at times, but we are blessed with some wonderful friends and family who have been so very supportive. I know that I would not have remained sane and intact without their back-up and I have come to appreciate my good friends even more than I did before. I can't begin to express how proud of Kim I am, how impressed I am, how in awe I am. It has been the worst time of our lives, but we have survived it and will continue to. We now have that normal life that I craved so much, albeit a new normal. In many ways we are in a better place than we were before cancer. I kept saying to myself, don't panic, it will all be OK, and it is.

Cancer cannot break us.
Cancer cannot stop us doing what we want to do.
Cancer cannot stop us having fun.
Cancer cannot stop us laughing.
Cancer cannot stop us loving.
Cancer cannot stop us living.
Cancer cannot have him - he's mine.

Postscript

How are you, Mr Ronaldson?

I'm pleased to say that I'm very well and looking forward to life, as I've always done. I get up and get going.

My health is good generally and my most recent scan revealed no new problems I hope that continues to be encouraging. Side effects are controlled and the 'new normal' is now very normal.

My company First Aid Development is picking up. I'm now a trained NLP and Hypnosis practitioner as well and have a second business, Kimnosis, with other projects on the go, such as this book. I'm also starting to do talks on behalf of the charity. The hypnotherapy is fascinating and I really enjoy helping people with that as a tool. I'm proud to say I'm a trustee of Topic of Cancer and I assist other charities as much as I can.

I have my good days and, just once in a while, I have a bad day. But don't we all? What's the prognosis? Very good as it stands.

I'd always wanted to write a book, but this was never meant to be the subject matter! So, keep an eye out, there's going to be another one soon.

For the moment, I hope you've enjoyed this book either as a story, as some advice or just an insight into my brilliant world.

30th June 2015

Thank you!

Kim and Hazel at Guildford Means Business 2015